MW00786174

Contents

Library of Congress Cataloging-in-Publication Data The heritage village collection. Dickens' village series.
p. cm. ISBN 0-86573-850-5 1. Cross-stitch--Patterns. 2. Villages in art. I. Cy DeCosse Incorporated.
TT778.C76H53 1996 746.46'041--dc20 96-18879

INTRODUCTION

Since 1977, when Department 56®, Inc. introduced its first
miniature lighted houses and churches, this leading designer of
fine collectibles has created whole villages of charming, hand-painted
porcelain buildings that reflect the warmth and joy of the Christmas season.
The Heritage Village Collection® is a delight to all who have made these irre-
sistible shops, cottages and churches part of their Christmas tradition.

Whether you own any of these items, give them as gifts, or just admire them and love to
stitch, you will appreciate seeing your favorite pieces translated into cross stitch. Each pattern
has been converted directly from the architectural drawings created by the skilled artisans of
Department 56.

The fifteen patterns presented here were selected from the almost one hundred Dickens' Village®
buildings issued from 1984 to the present. The designs reflect the bustling, hearty, joyous atmos-
phere of Victorian England. With the exception of a few intentional reproductions, such as "Victoria
Station" and "The Old Curiosity Shop," all the buildings are completely original designs, based on
extensive research.

Whichever building you choose to begin with, use the box labeled *Personal Notes* to record a stitching
history for each pattern – when you began and finished it; the name of the recipient, if you made it
as a gift; and any stitching information you want to remember. Your stitched Dickens' Village pieces
can decorate your home all year long, or become the beginning of a lovely new Christmas tradition
for you, your family and friends.

RUTH MARION SCOTCH WOOLENS

FINISHED DESIGN SIZE: 10 5/8" X 9"
FRAME SIZE: 20" X 19"

RUTH MARION SCOTCH WOOLENS

ISSUED in 1989   RETIRED in 1990

Limited Edition
17,500

Flannels and worsteds, tweeds and tartans
Woven with tender care.
Whether vests or sweaters, jackets or caps
In colors blended with flair.
For autumn days on Yorkshire dales,
There's nothing better to wear.

PERSONAL *Notes*

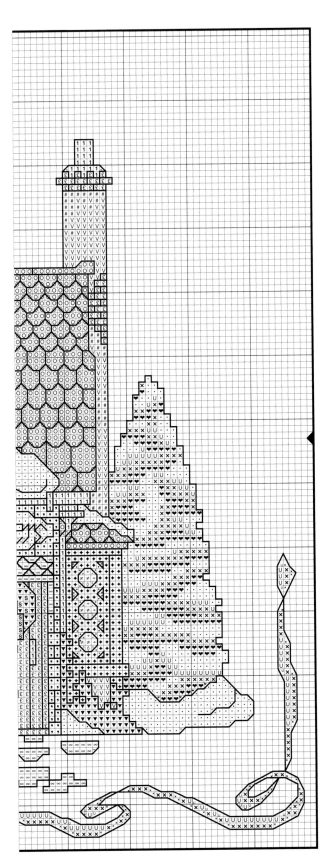

RUTH MARION SCOTCH WOOLENS
p a t t e r n

COLOR KEY

SYMBOL	COLOR	DMC	ANCHOR
•	White	000	2
1	Pewter Gray	317	400
s	Christmas Red	321	9046
❤	Vy. Dk. Blue Green	500	683
x	Dk. Blue Green	501	878
u	Blue Green	502	877
v	Ultra Vy. Lt. Beige Brown	543	933
◊	Med. Tangerine	741	304
≠	Med. Yellow	743	302
÷	Lt. Pale Yellow	745	300
♦	Dk. Beige Brown	839	360
o	Med. Beige Brown	840	379
#	Vy. Lt. Beige Brown	842	388
▼	Dk. Emerald Green	910	229
'	Med. Golden Brown	976	1001
∞	Dk. Pine Green	3362	263
£	Terra Cotta	3830	5975

special instructions

Refer to pages 94-95 for general stitching information. Use 2 strands of floss for cross stitches and 1 strand for backstitches, unless otherwise noted.

BLENDED STITCHES

" {	Med. Old Gold (2 str)	729	890
	Gold blending filament (1 str)	002BF	002BF

BACKSTITCHES

—	Black (2 str) - Shop names	310	403
—	Lt. Steel Gray - All snow and ice	318	399
—	Vy. Dk. Blue Green - All trees and borders	500	683
—	Black Brown - All else	3371	382

Fabric: 14-count natural Aida
Stitch Count: 152 wide × 131 high

T. WELLS FRUIT & SPICE SHOP

FINISHED DESIGN: 8½" X 10⅛"
FRAME SIZE: 18" X 20¼"

Dickens' Village Series

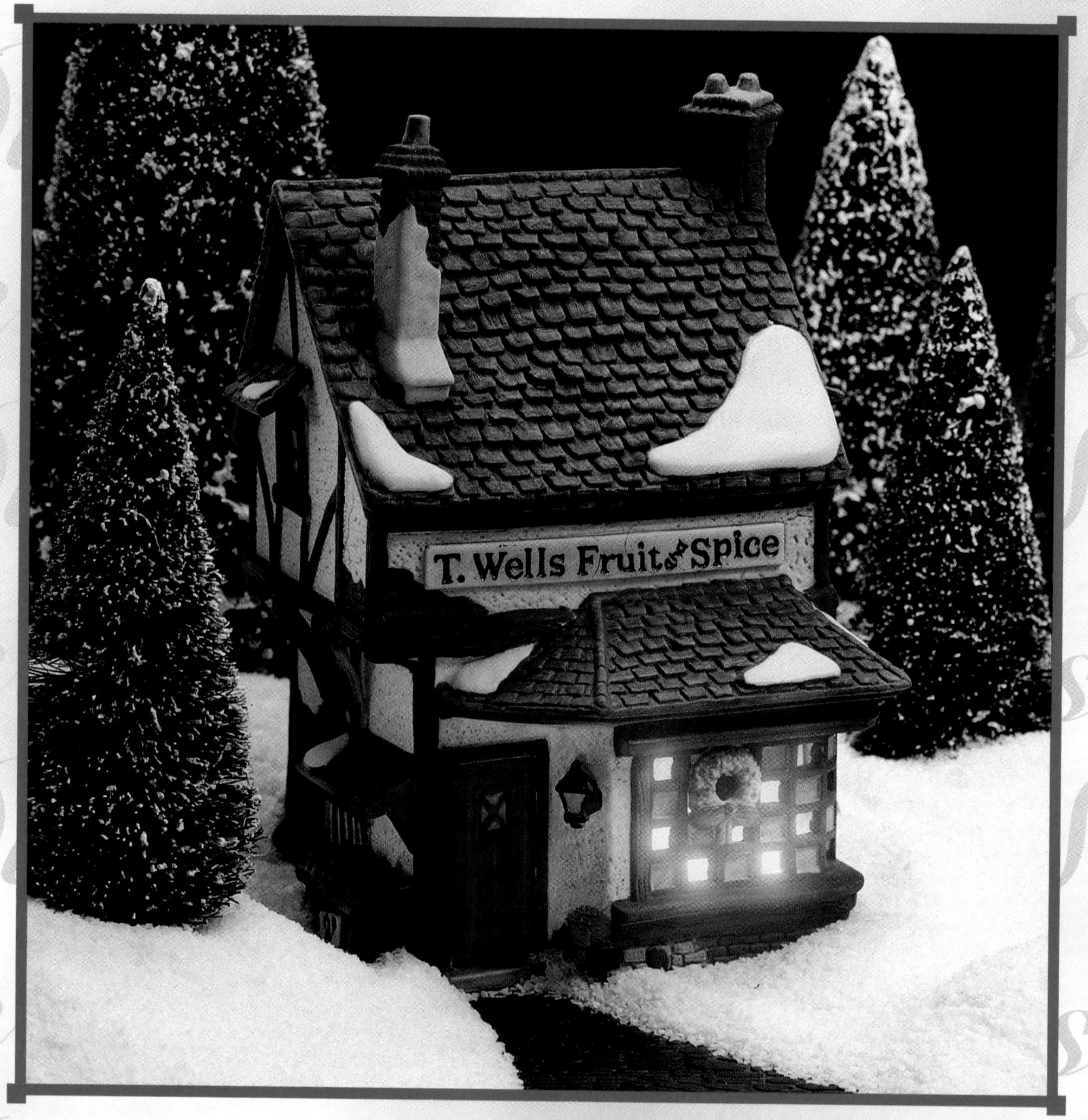

T. WELLS FRUIT & SPICE SHOP
ISSUED in 1988   RETIRED in 1990

The fruit and spice shop lures us in
With tantalizing scents—
Exotic wares from far-off lands
And homely condiments.
Cinnamon, nutmeg, mace and cloves
For pound cakes, fruitcakes, scones and loaves.
Peppers, mustards, herbs to grind,
Apples, pears of every kind—

And for a special Christmas treat,
A pineapple or orange sweet.

PERSONAL *Notes*

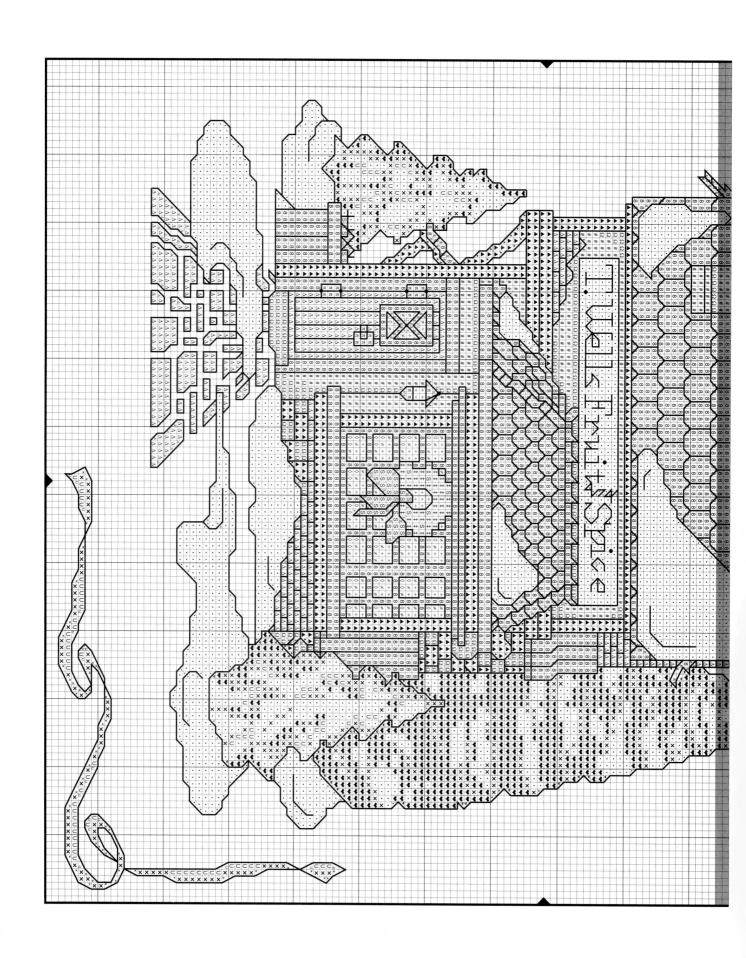

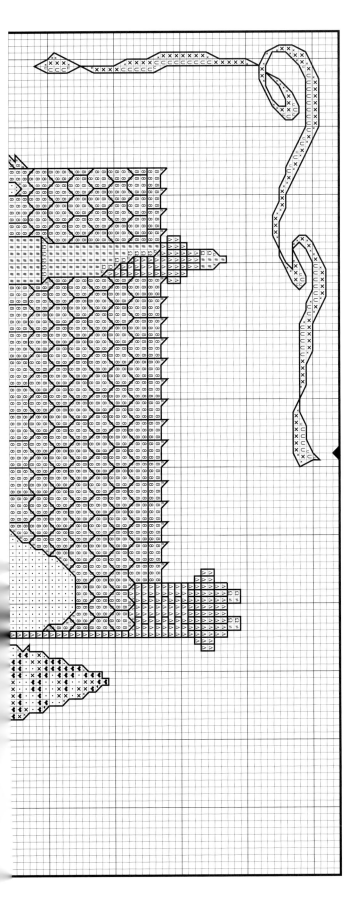

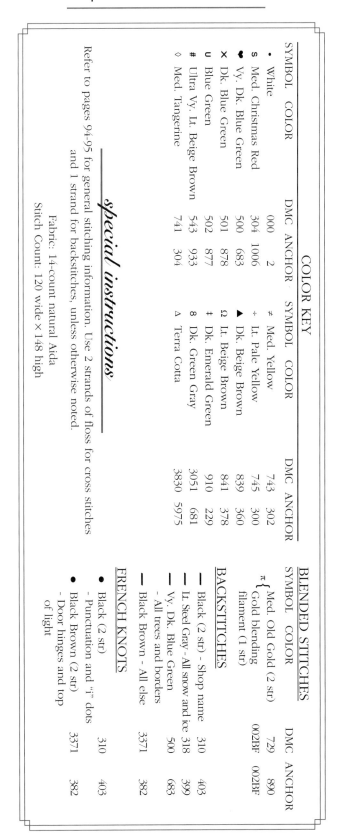

COLOR KEY

SYMBOL	COLOR	DMC	ANCHOR
•	White	000	2
s	Med. Christmas Red	304	1006
♥	Vy. Dk. Blue Green	500	683
×	Dk. Blue Green	501	878
u	Blue Green	502	877
#	Ultra Vy. Lt. Beige Brown	543	933
◊	Med. Tangerine	741	304

SYMBOL	COLOR	DMC	ANCHOR
≠	Med. Yellow	743	302
+	Lt. Pale Yellow	745	300
▲	Dk. Beige Brown	839	360
Ω	Lt. Beige Brown	841	378
†	Dk. Emerald Green	910	229
8	Dk. Green Gray	3051	681
△	Terra Cotta	3830	5975

BLENDED STITCHES

SYMBOL	COLOR	DMC	ANCHOR
π {	Med. Old Gold (2 str)	729	890
{	Gold blending filament (1 str)	002BF	002BF

BACKSTITCHES

	COLOR	DMC	ANCHOR
—	Black (2 str) - Shop name	310	403
—	Lt. Steel Gray - All snow and ice	318	399
—	Vy. Dk. Blue Green - All trees and borders	500	683
—	Black Brown - All else	3371	382

FRENCH KNOTS

	COLOR	DMC	ANCHOR
•	Black (2 str) - Punctuation and "i" dots	310	403
•	Black Brown (2 str) - Door hinges and top of light	3371	382

special instructions

Refer to pages 94-95 for general stitching information. Use 2 strands of floss for cross stitches and 1 strand for backstitches, unless otherwise noted.

Fabric: 14-count natural Aida
Stitch Count: 120 wide × 148 high

LOMAS LTD. MOLASSES

FINISHED DESIGN SIZE: 8 1/2" X 8 7/8"
FRAME SIZE: 17 3/4" X 18 3/4"

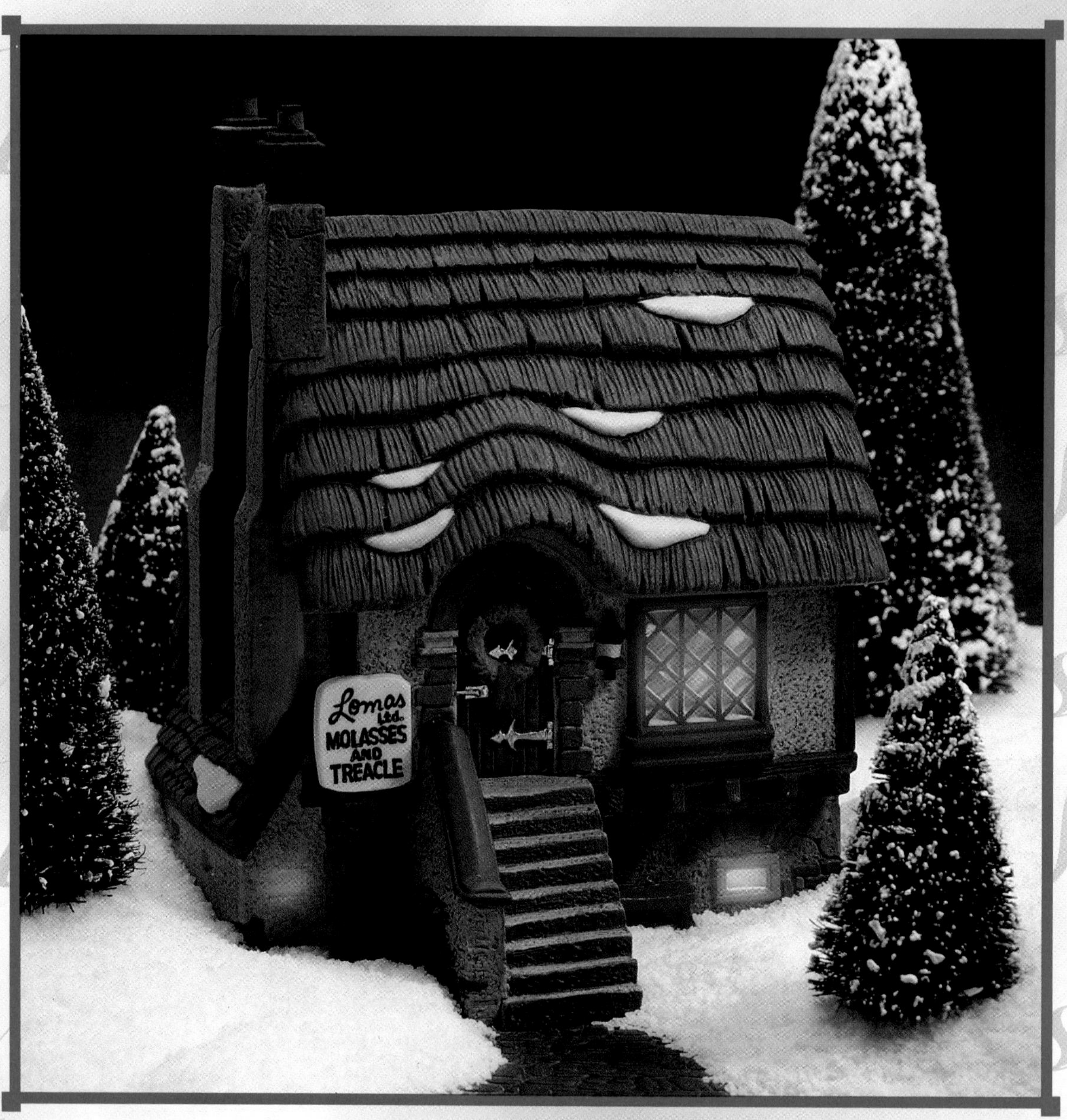
Lomas Ltd.
MOLASSES AND TREACLE

LOMAS LTD. MOLASSES

ISSUED in 1993   CURRENT

Molasses and treacle are treats for the poor,
Used on pudding and bread.
Country folk use honey from bees,
The wealthy, fine sugar instead.

Half a pound of tuppenny rice,
Would not seem such a treat
Without the treacle added in
To make the mealtime sweet.

PERSONAL *Notes*

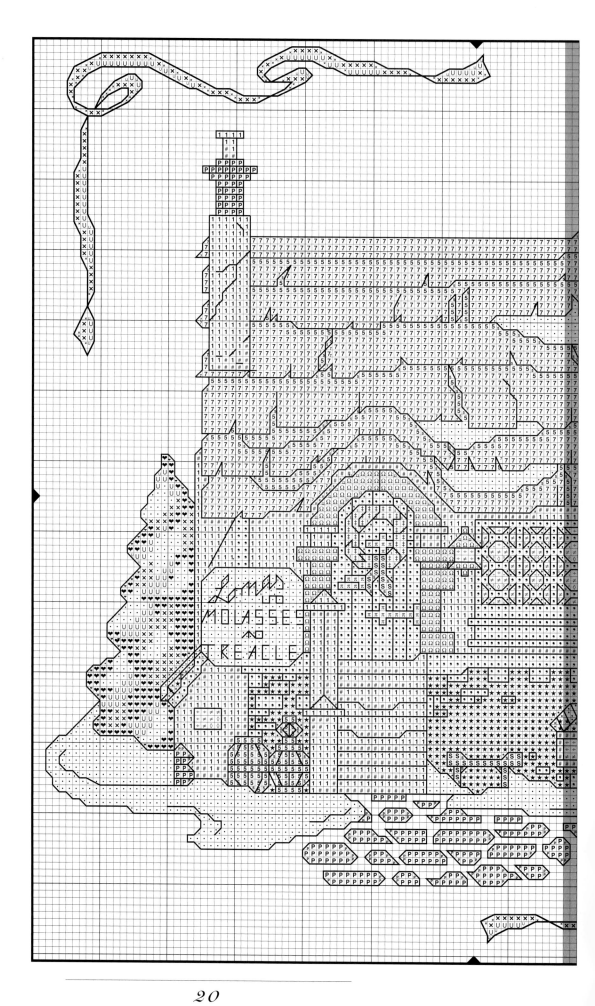

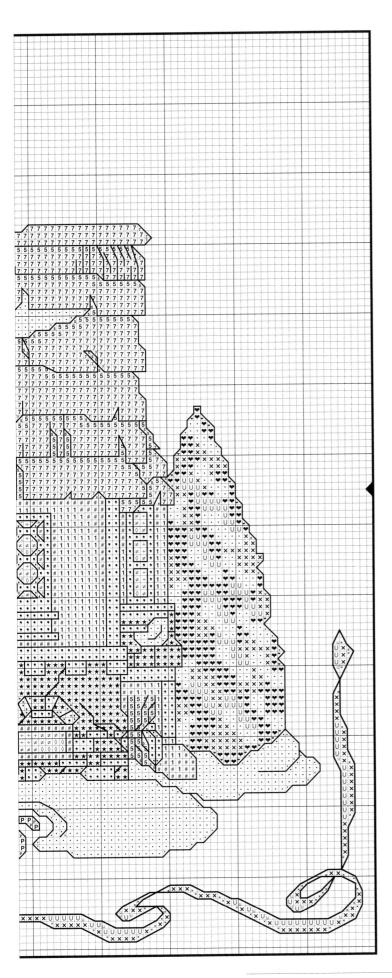

LOMAS LTD. MOLASSES
p a t t e r n

COLOR KEY

SYMBOL	COLOR	DMC	ANCHOR
•	White	000	2
s	Christmas Red	321	9046
P	Dk. Terra Cotta	355	1014
Ω	Dk. Steel Gray	414	235
5	Vy. Lt. Brown	435	1046
7	Lt. Tan	437	362
♥	Vy. Dk. Blue Green	500	683
x	Dk. Blue Green	501	878
U	Blue Green	502	877
1	Ultra Vy. Lt. Beige Brown	543	933
◊	Med. Tangerine	741	304
≠	Med. Yellow	743	302
✛	Lt. Pale Yellow	745	300
·	Dk. Beige Brown	839	360
#	Vy. Lt. Beige Brown	842	388
‡	Dk. Emerald Green	910	229
★	Med. Green Gray	3052	262

special instructions

Refer to pages 94-95 for general stitching information. Use 2 strands of floss for cross stitches and 1 strand for backstitches, unless otherwise noted.

BLENDED STITCHES

π {	Med. Old Gold (2 str)	729	890
	Gold blending filament (1 str)	002BF	002BF

BACKSTITCHES

—	Black (2 str)	310	403
	- Shop name		
—	Lt. Steel Gray	318	399
	- All snow and ice		
—	Vy. Dk. Blue Green	500	683
	- All trees and borders		
—	Black Brown	3371	382
	- All else		

Fabric: 14-count natural Aida
Stitch Count: 126 wide × 128 high

BISHOPS OAST HOUSE

FINISHED DESIGN SIZE: 8 7/8" X 9 3/8"
FRAME SIZE: 18" X 19"

Dickens' Village Series

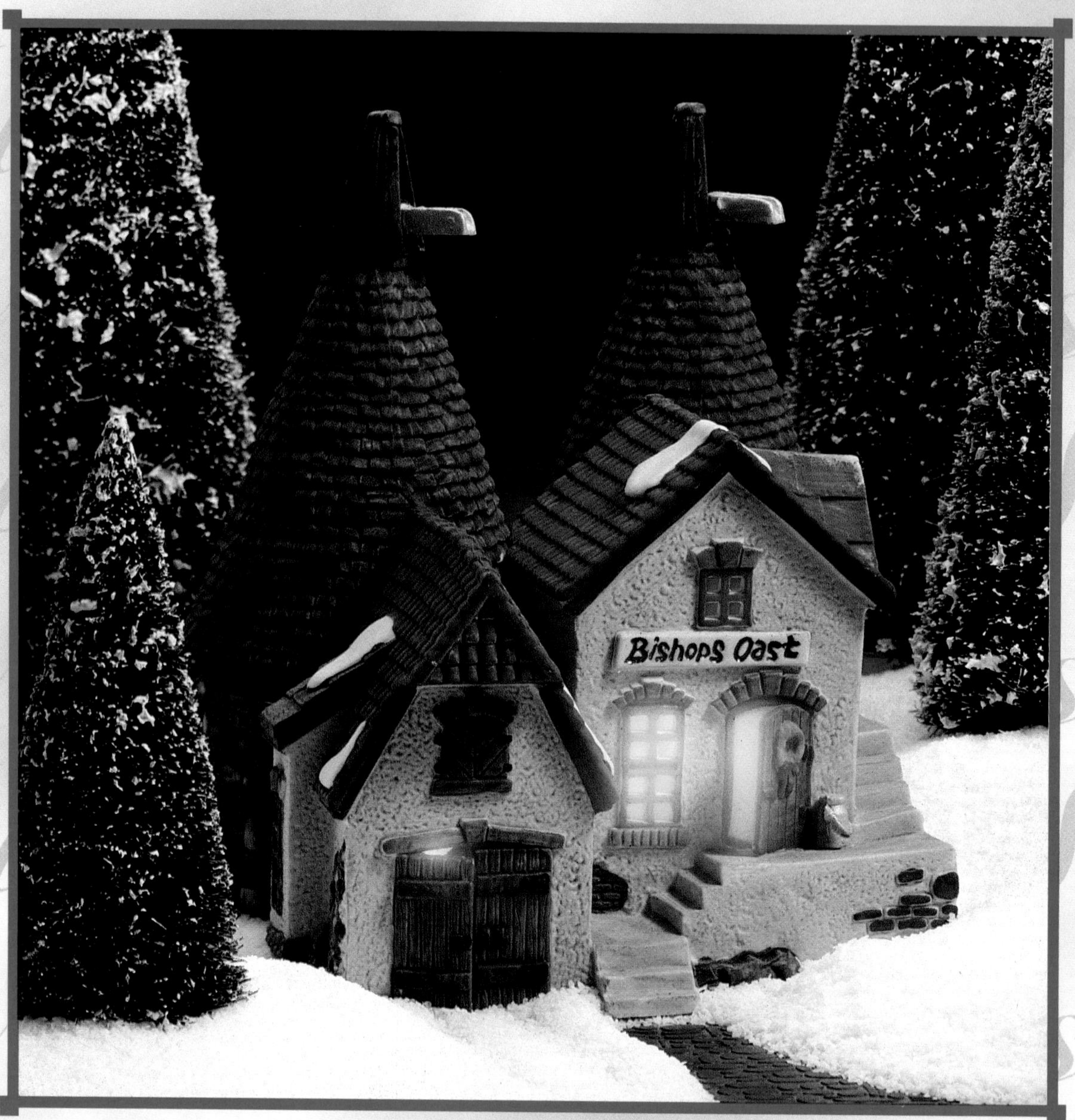

BISHOPS OAST HOUSE

ISSUED in 1990   RETIRED in 1992

The harvest is brought to Bishops oast,
'Round the clock the hops do roast.
Shovel coal,
Stoke the fire,
Tend the kilns
Never tire.
The brewers are waiting this year's crop,
To make fine ales for every shop.

PERSONAL *Notes*

_____
_____
_____
_____
_____
_____
_____
_____
_____
_____

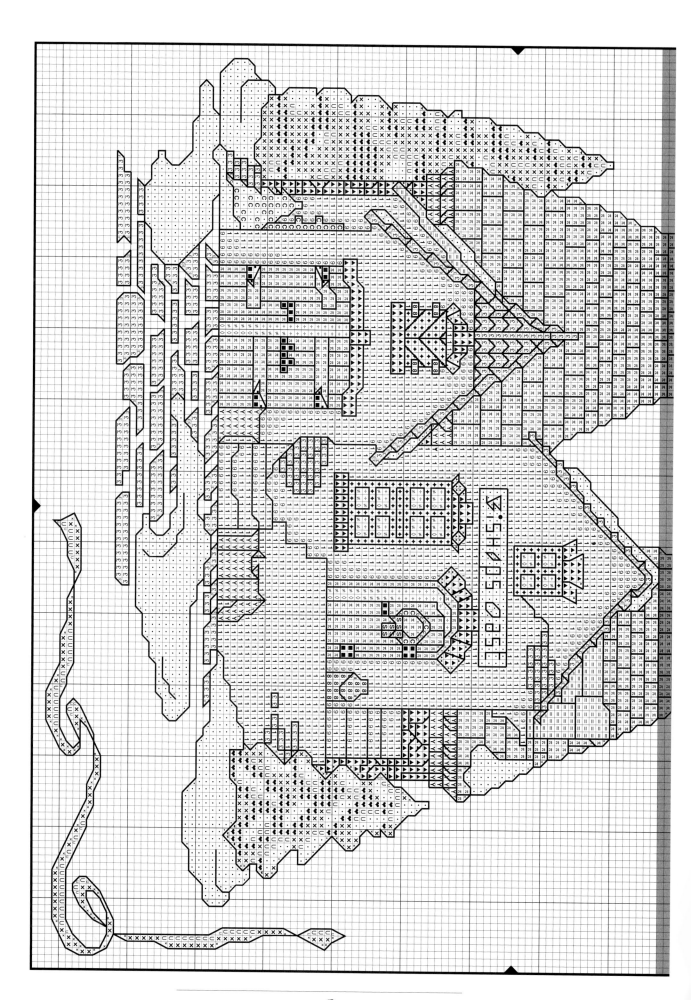

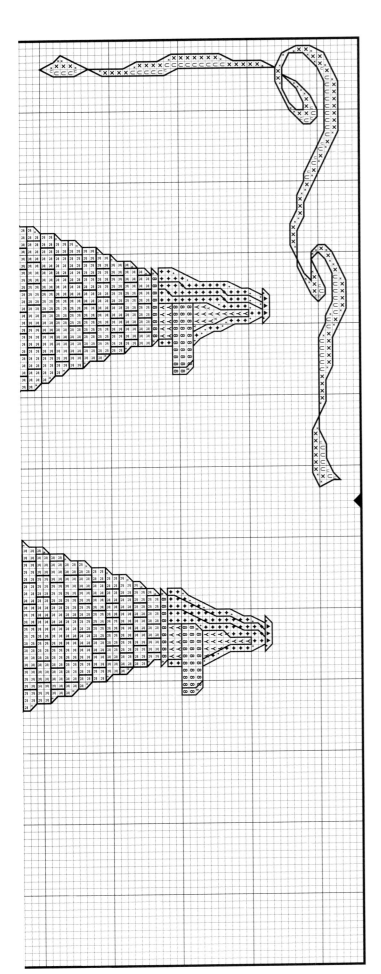

BISHOPS OAST HOUSE
p a t t e r n

COLOR KEY

SYMBOL	COLOR	DMC	ANCHOR	SYMBOL	COLOR	DMC	ANCHOR
•	White	000	2	9	Ultra Vy. Lt. Tan	739	387
s	Med. Christmas Red	304	1006	◊	Med. Tangerine	741	304
■	Black	310	403	≠	Med. Yellow	743	302
▲	Dk. Shell Gray	451	233	+	Lt. Pale Yellow	745	300
♥	Vy. Dk. Blue Green	500	683	c	Dk. Emerald Green	910	229
×	Dk. Blue Green	501	878	=	Dk. Khaki Green	3011	846
u	Blue Green	502	877	π	Dk. Rose Brown	3772	1007
◆	Vy. Dk. Rose Brown	632	936	Y	Vy. Dk. Pink Beige	3773	1008
1	Cream	712	926	&	Terra Cotta	3830	5975

BLENDED STITCHES

SYMBOL	COLOR	DMC	ANCHOR
8 {	Pearl Gray (2 str)	415	398
	Silver blending filament (1 str)	001BF	001BF

BACKSTITCHES

—	Black (2 str) - Oast name	310	403
—	Black - Around silver blended metallic stitches	310	403
—	Lt. Steel Gray - All snow and ice	318	399
—	Vy. Dk. Blue Green - All trees and borders	500	683
—	Black Brown - All else	3371	382

FRENCH KNOTS

•	Black (2 str) -"i" dot on sign	310	403

special instructions

Refer to pages 94-95 for general stitching information. Use 2 strands of floss for cross stitches and 1 strand for backstitches, unless otherwise noted.

Fabric: 14-count natural Aida
Stitch Count: 130 wide × 140 high

GREEN GATE COTTAGE

FINISHED DESIGN SIZE: 7 3/4" x 10 1/2"
FRAME SIZE: 18" x 21"

GREEN GATE COTTAGE

ISSUED in 1989   RETIRED in 1990

Limited Edition
22,500

Tall and thin, a little off center,
It's definitely not symmetric.
With chimneys galore and different styles,
You could almost say it's eccentric.

A fire crackles in every room,
The windows are aglow with light.
The family is together again
On this frosty winter's night.

PERSONAL *Notes*

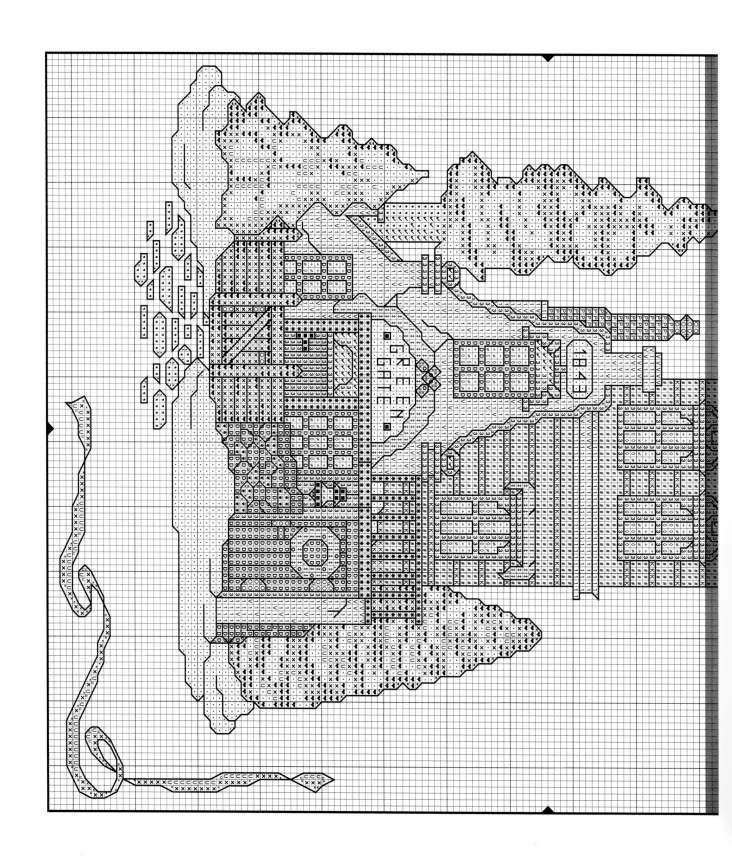

GREEN GATE COTTAGE
pattern

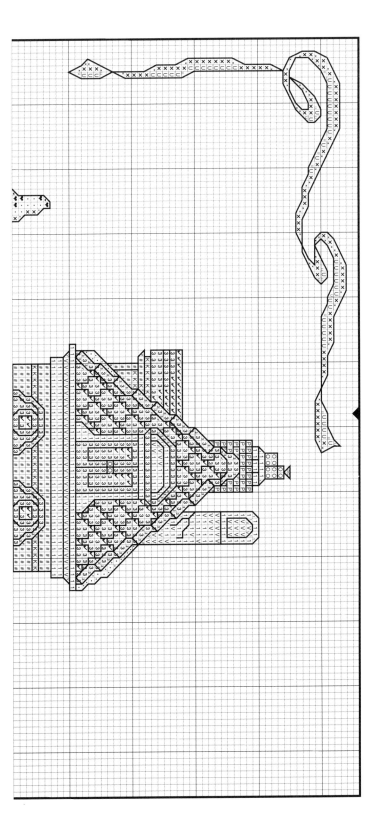

COLOR KEY

SYMBOL	COLOR	DMC	ANCHOR
•	White	000	2
1	Ecru	Ecru	387
■	Black	310	403
P	Dk. Terra Cotta	355	1014
❂	Dk. Christmas Red	498	1005
♣	Vy. Dk. Blue Green	500	683
✗	Dk. Blue Green	501	878
u	Blue Green	502	877
v	Ultra Vy. Lt. Beige Brown	543	933
D	Dk. Beige Gray	642	392
◊	Med. Tangerine	741	304

SYMBOL	COLOR	DMC	ANCHOR
≠	Med. Yellow	743	302
+	Lt. Pale Yellow	745	300
•	Dk. Coffee Brown	801	359
✦	Vy. Dk. Beige Brown	838	380
K	Lt. Beige Brown	841	378
#	Vy. Lt. Beige Brown	842	388
✓	Dk. Golden Brown	975	355
‡	Dk. Emerald Green	910	229
✔	Ultra Dk. Beige Gray	3790	393
O	Vy. Dk. Pewter Gray	3799	236
3	Golden Brown	3826	1049

special instructions

Refer to pages 94-95 for general stitching information. Use 2 strands of floss for cross stitches and 1 strand for backstitches, unless otherwise noted.

BACKSTITCHES

SYMBOL	COLOR	DMC	ANCHOR
—	Black (2 Str) - House name and date	310	403
—	Black - Hinges, doorknobs, lantern and chimneys	310	403
—	Lt. Steel Gray - All snow and ice	318	399
—	Vy. Dk. Blue Green - All trees and borders	500	683
—	Black Brown - All else	3371	382

Fabric: 14-count natural Aida
Stitch Count: 113 wide × 156 high

VICTORIA STATION

FINISHED DESIGN SIZE: 15 3/8" X 10 3/4"
FRAME SIZE: 25 1/2" X 21 1/2"

VICTORIA STATION

ISSUED in 1989   CURRENT

Billows of steam and whistle's scream
In the station called Victoria.
The granite queen conducts the scene
Of traveller's euphoria.
She stands and waits and bids adieu
To each and every one of you.

PERSONAL *Notes*

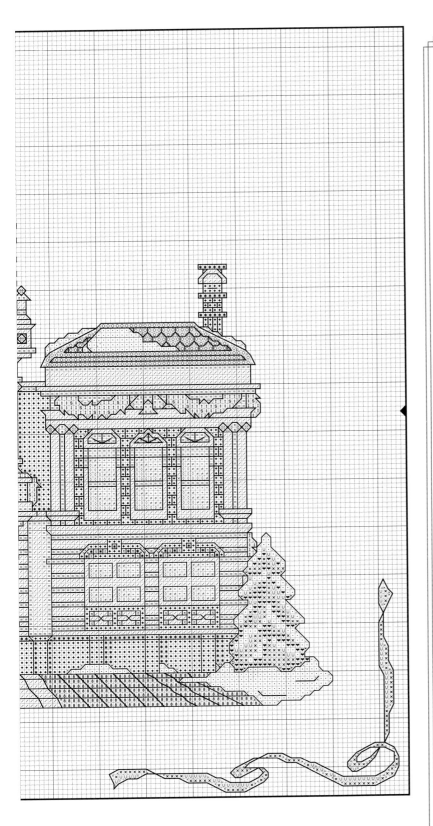

COLOR KEY

SYMBOL	COLOR	DMC	ANCHOR
•	White	000	2
s	Med. Christmas Red	304	1006
✦	Dk. Pewter Gray	413	401
❤	Vy. Dk. Blue Green	500	683
✕	Dk. Blue Green	501	878
u	Blue Green	502	877
◊	Med. Tangerine	741	304
≠	Med. Yellow	743	302
÷	Lt. Pale Yellow	745	300
‡	Dk. Emerald Green	910	229
o	Med. Copper	920	1004
/	Vy. Lt. Mocha Brown	3033	391
=	Lt. Mocha Brown	3782	899
✳	Vy. Dk. Pewter Gray	3799	236
8	Terra Cotta	3830	5975

special instructions

Refer to pages 94-95 for general stitching information. Use 2 strands of floss for cross stitches and 1 strand for backstitches, unless otherwise noted.

BLENDED STITCHES

π {	Med. Old Gold (2 str)	729	890
	Gold blending filament (1 str)	002BF	002BF

BACKSTITCHES

—	Black	310	403
	- Station name and clock hands		
—	Lt. Steel Gray	318	399
	- All snow and ice		
—	Vy. Dk. Blue Green	500	683
	- All trees and borders		
—	Black Brown	3371	382
	- All else		

FRENCH KNOTS

•	Black (2 str)	310	403
	- Clock numbers		

Fabric: 14-count natural Aida
Stitch Count: 223 wide × 156 high

W.M. WHEAT CAKES & PUDDINGS

FINISHED DESIGN SIZE: 7 3/4" x 10 5/8"
FRAME SIZE: 16 3/4" x 20"

Dickens' Village Series

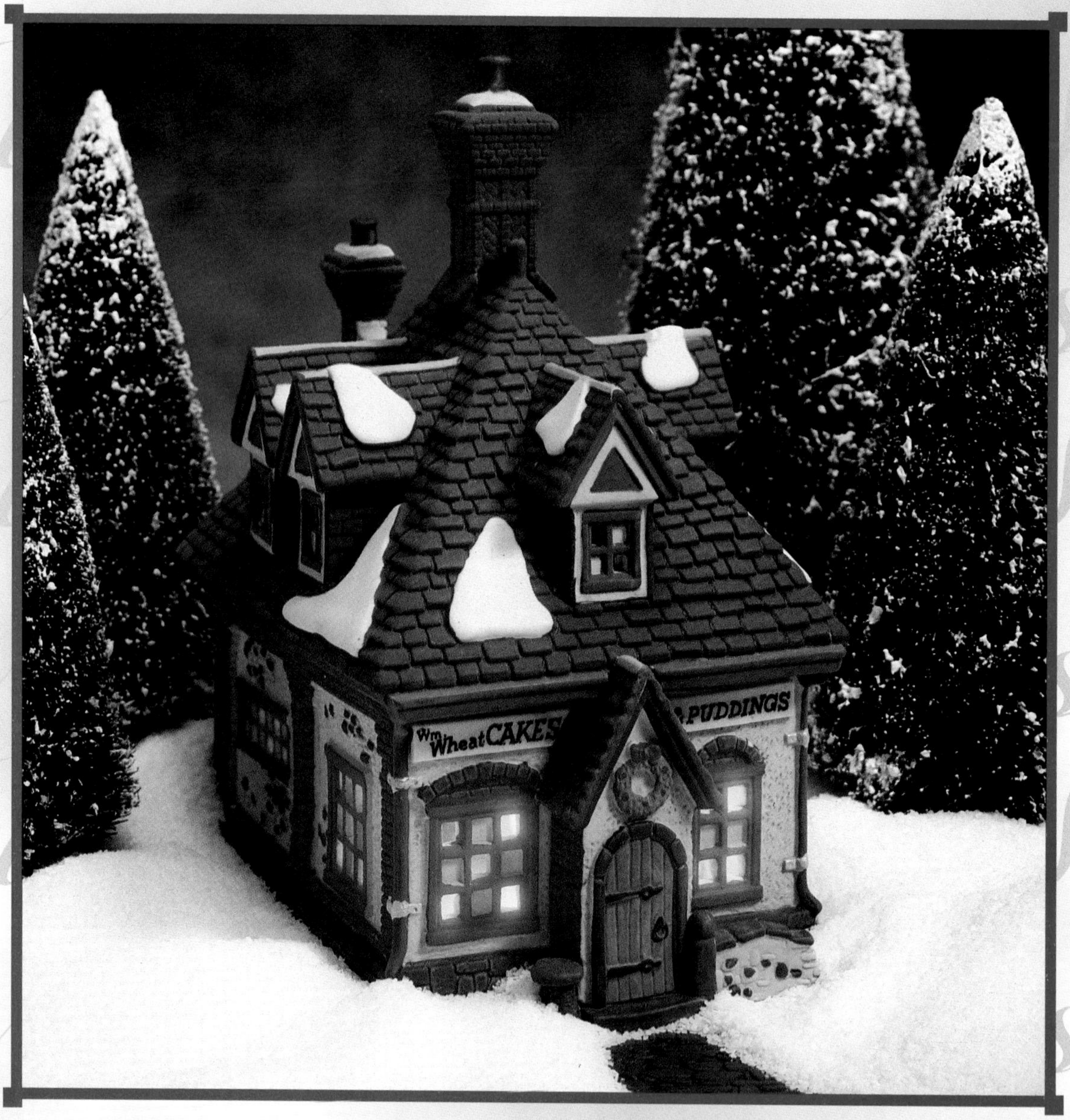

W.M. WHEAT CAKES & PUDDINGS

ISSUED in 1993   CURRENT

Each year, the master of the house,
The Christmas pudding serves—
Full of currants, dark and sweet,
We've just what he deserves.

Take home our fine plum pudding,
Our cakes and muffins too.
Sweet biscuits for the little ones
Will make their dreams come true.

PERSONAL *Notes*

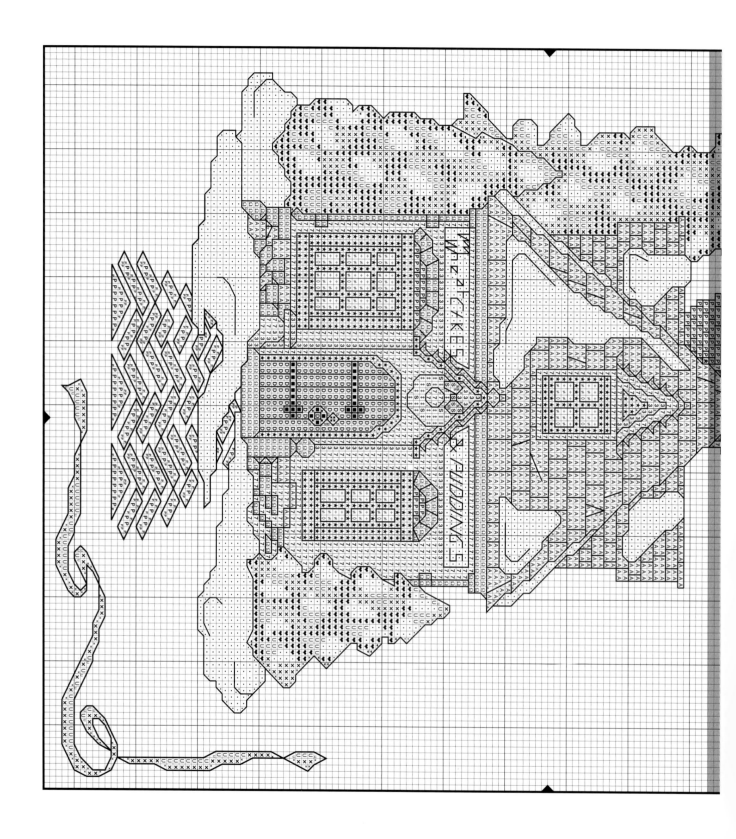

COLOR KEY

SYMBOL	COLOR	DMC	ANCHOR	SYMBOL	COLOR	DMC	ANCHOR
•	White	000	2	×	Dk. Blue Green	501	878
s	Med. Christmas Red	304	1006	u	Blue Green	502	877
■	Black	310	403	◇	Med. Tangerine	741	304
3	Lt. Steel Gray	318	399	≠	Med. Yellow	743	302
3	Dk. Terra Cotta	355	1014	÷	Lt. Pale Yellow	745	300
P	Med. Terra Cotta	356	5975	A	Dk. Beige Brown	839	360
D	Dk. Steel Gray	414	235	‡	Dk. Emerald Green	910	229
Ω	Pearl Gray	415	398	★	Med. Green Gray	3052	262
7	Vy. Dk. Blue Green	500	683				

BACKSTITCHES

SYMBOL	COLOR	DMC	ANCHOR
—	Black (2 str) - Shop name	310	403
—	Lt. Steel Gray - All snow and ice	318	399
—	Vy. Dk. Blue Green - All trees and borders	500	683
—	Black Brown - All else	3371	382

Fabric: 14-count natural Aida
Stitch Count: 112 wide × 159 high

special instructions

Refer to pages 94-95 for general stitching information. Use 2 strands of floss for cross stitches and 1 strand for backstitches, unless otherwise noted.

THE OLD CURIOSITY SHOP

FINISHED DESIGN SIZE: 12 ½" x 8½"
FRAME SIZE: 22" x 18½"

THE OLD CURIOSITY SHOP

ISSUED in 1987   CURRENT

Come in and browse; then stay all day,
We've many wonders to sell:
Queer carvings, armor, furniture and rugs,
Ancient books with magic spells.
And hidden amidst the musty wares
Memories of little Nell.

PERSONAL *Notes*

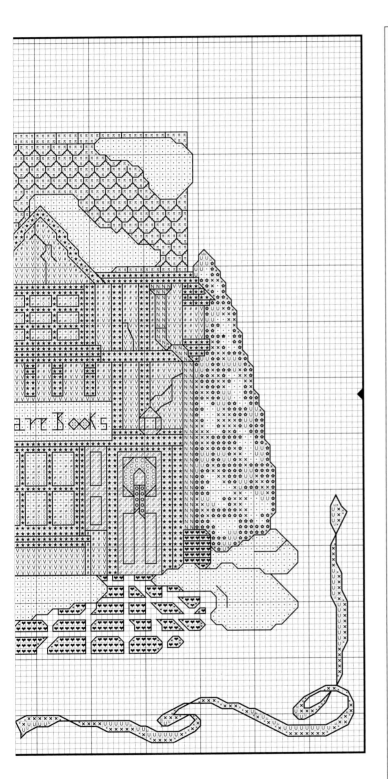

COLOR KEY

SYMBOL	COLOR	DMC	ANCHOR
•	White	000	2
■	Black	310	403
N	Pewter Gray	317	400
✪	Dk. Christmas Red	498	1005
✿	Vy. Dk. Blue Green	500	683
✕	Dk. Blue Green	501	878
U	Blue Green	502	877
V	Ultra Vy. Lt. Beige Brown	543	933
◊	Lt. Tangerine	742	303
≠	Med. Yellow	743	302
÷	Lt. Pale Yellow	745	300
π	Dk. Coffee Brown	801	359
♥	Dk. Beige Brown	839	360
//	Med. Beige Brown	840	379
#	Vy. Lt. Beige Brown	842	388
c	Dk. Emerald Green	910	229
s	Dk. Red Copper	918	341
P	Dk. Antique Blue	930	1035
★	Golden Brown	3826	1049

special instructions

Refer to pages 94-95 for general stitching
information. Use 2 strands of floss for cross
stitches and 1 strand for backstitches,
unless otherwise noted.

BACKSTITCHES

— Black (2 str) - Shop names,	310	403
signs and date		
— Lt. Steel Gray	318	399
- All snow and ice		
— Vy. Dk. Blue Green	500	683
- All trees and borders		
— Black Brown	3371	382
- All else		

Fabric: 14-count natural Aida
Stitch Count: 182 wide × 124 high

COBB COTTAGE

FINISHED DESIGN SIZE: 9¾" X 8⅛"
FRAME SIZE: 19⅞" X 18¾"

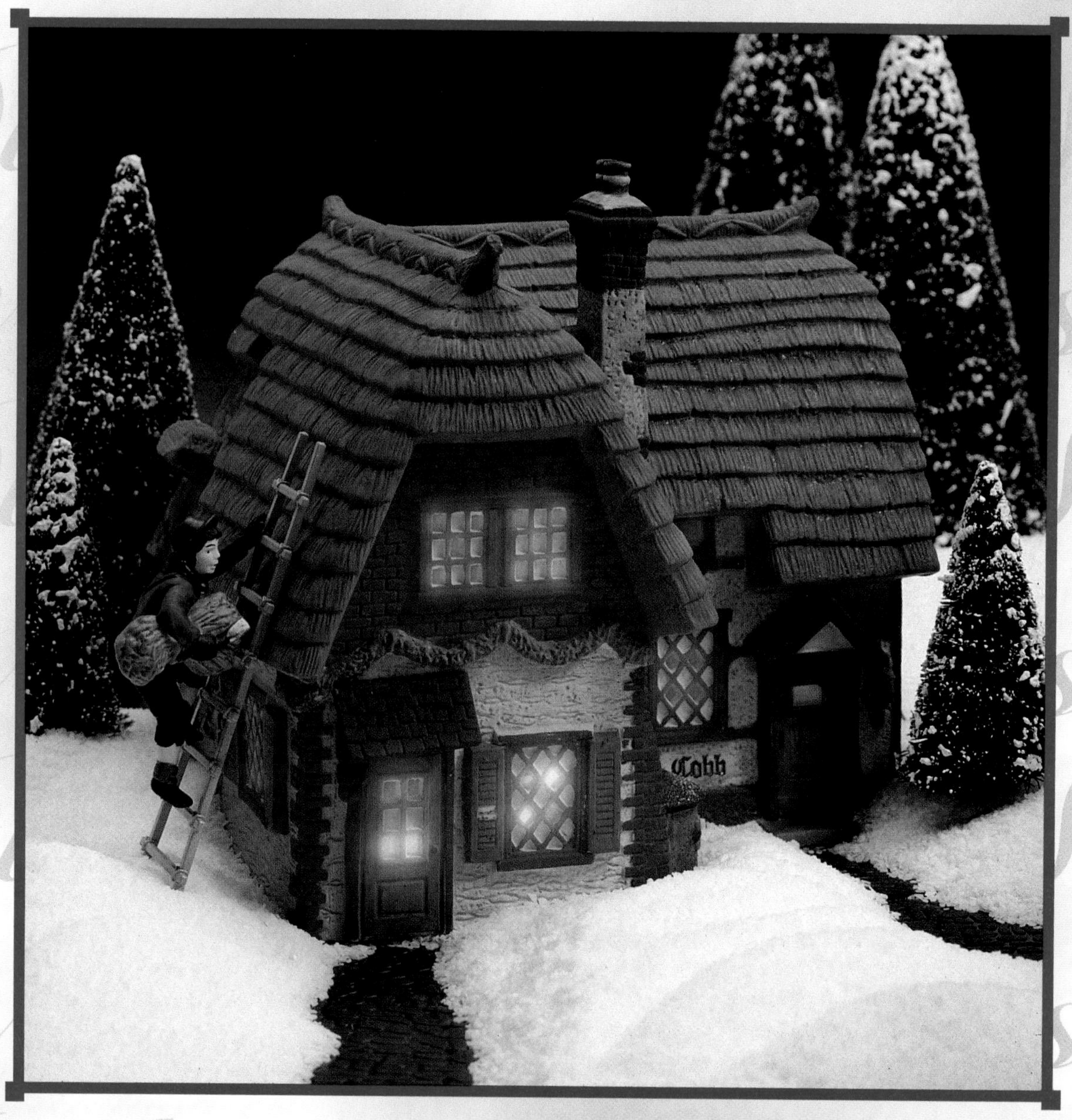
Cobb

COBB COTTAGE

ISSUED in 1994   CURRENT

Brush off the snow, put up the ladder;
The thatchers begin their job,
Down along Portobello Road
Atop a cottage called Cobb.

Hoist a bundle, begin the ascent,
Fresh thatch will keep out the cold.
It will look its absolute best
With a shiny new roof of gold.

PERSONAL *Notes*

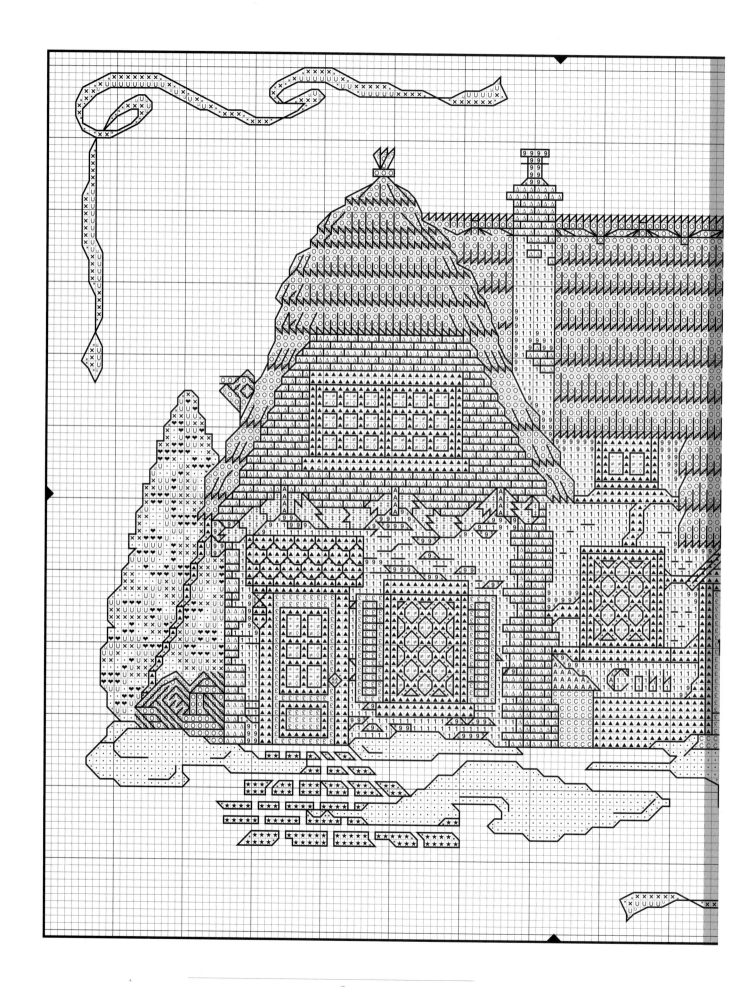

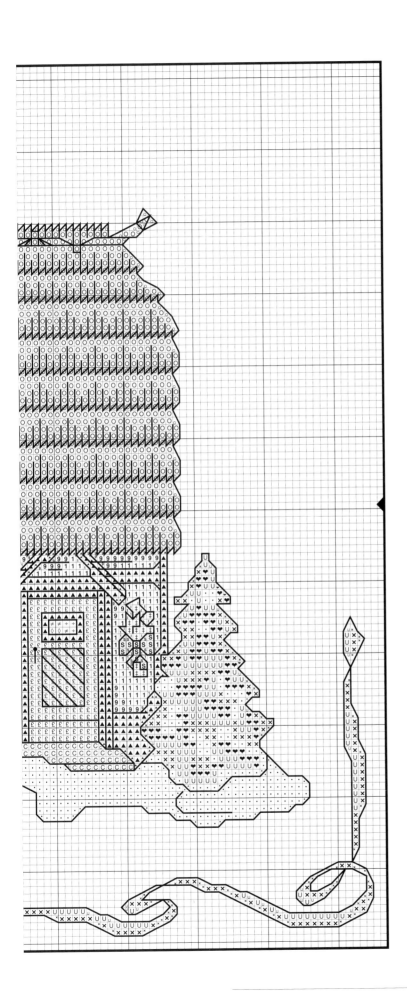

COLOR KEY			
SYMBOL	COLOR	DMC	ANCHOR
•	White	000	2
s	Med. Christmas Red	304	1006
c	Lt. Steel Gray	318	399
A	Dk. Pewter Gray	413	401
£	Avocado Green	469	267
♥	Vy. Dk. Blue Green	500	683
×	Dk. Blue Green	501	878
U	Blue Green	502	877
◊	Med. Tangerine	741	304
≠	Med. Yellow	743	302
÷	Lt. Pale Yellow	745	300
▲	Dk. Beige Brown	839	360
‡	Dk. Emerald Green	910	229
★	Vy. Dk. Avocado Green	936	269
9	Med. Mocha Brown	3032	903
1	Lt. Mocha Brown	3782	899
o	Vy. Dk. Old Gold	3829	901
△	Terra Cotta	3830	5975

special instructions

Refer to pages 94-95 for general stitching information. Use 2 strands of floss for cross stitches and 1 strand for backstitches, unless otherwise noted.

BACKSTITCHES

—	Black (2 str)	310	403
	- Cottage name		
—	Lt. Steel Gray	318	399
	- All snow and ice		
—	Vy. Dk. Blue Green	500	683
	- All trees and borders		
—	Black Brown	3371	382
	- All else		

FRENCH KNOTS

•	Black (2 str)	310	403
	- Door handle		

Fabric: 14-count natural Aida
Stitch Count: 141 wide × 119 high

FAGIN'S HIDE-A-WAY

FINISHED DESIGN SIZE: 93/8" X 9"
FRAME SIZE: 191/4" X 193/8"

Dickens' Village Series

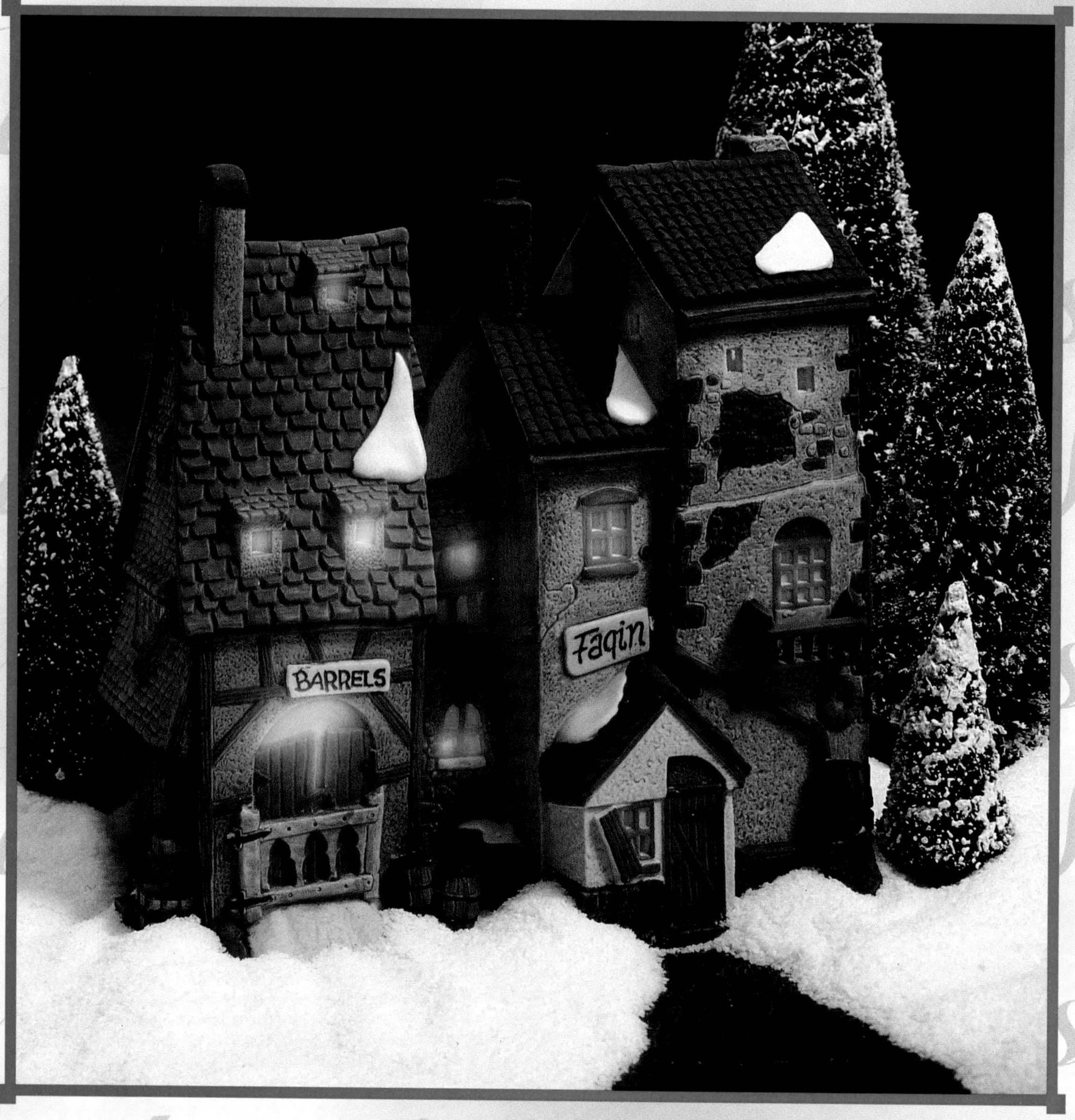

FAGIN'S HIDE-A-WAY

ISSUED in 1991   RETIRED in 1995

Fagin is a fingersmith,
And nimble are his boys.
He sends them forth to pocket pick,
An army he deploys.

Watches, hankies, silks and wallets,
Are the plundered loot.
Stolen by a troupe of boys,
Costumed in tattered suit.

PERSONAL *Notes*

_____
_____
_____
_____
_____
_____
_____
_____
_____
_____

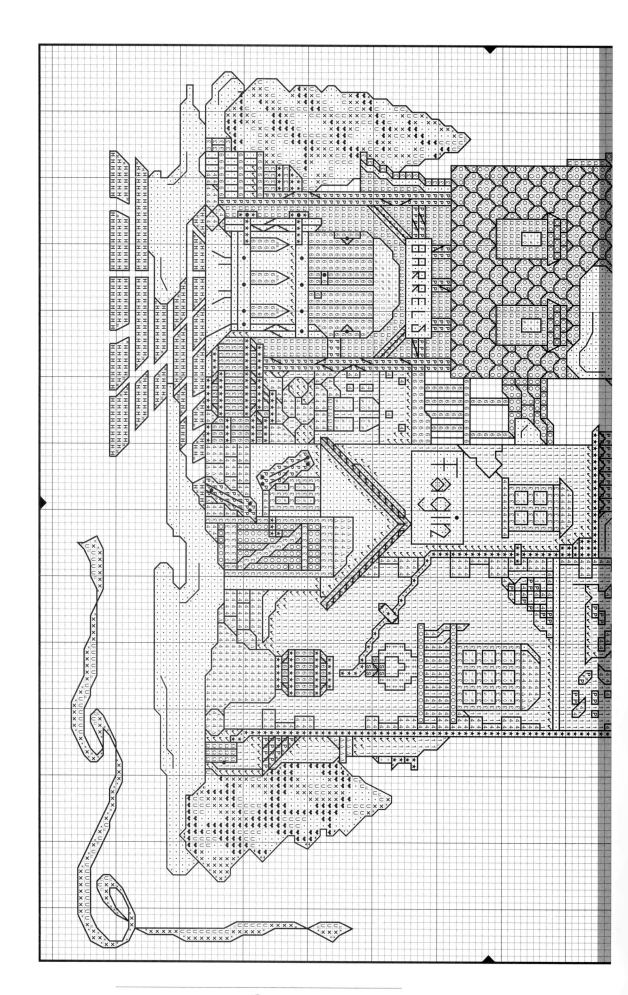

FAGIN'S HIDE-A-WAY
p a t t e r n

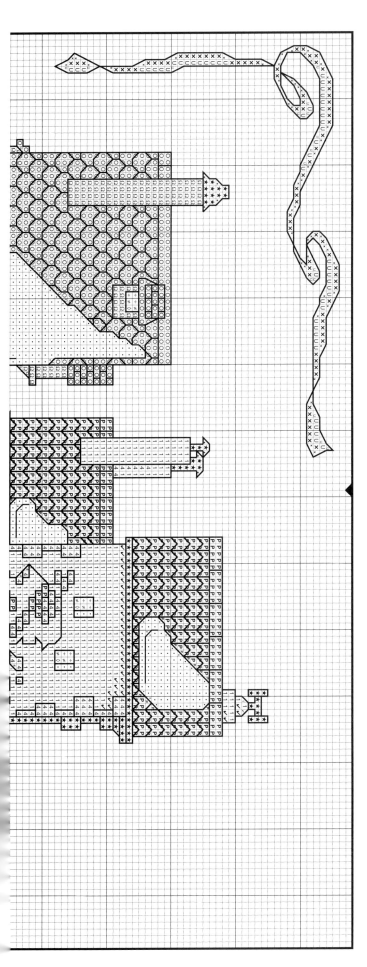

COLOR KEY

SYMBOL	COLOR	DMC	ANCHOR	SYMBOL	COLOR	DMC	ANCHOR
•	White	000	2	u	Blue Green	502	877
P	Vy. Dk. Shell Pink	221	897	✔	Med. Beaver Gray	647	1040
H	Vy. Dk. Mahogany	300	352	ι	Lt. Beaver Gray	648	900
s	Med. Christmas Red	304	1006	◇	Med. Tangerine	741	304
△	Pewter Gray	317	400	≠	Med. Yellow	743	302
6	Med. Terra Cotta	356	5975	÷	Lt. Pale Yellow	745	300
★	Dk. Pewter Gray	413	401	‡	Dk. Emerald Green	910	229
4	Dk. Steel Gray	414	235	Ω	Dk. Avocado Green	936	269
♥	Vy. Dk. Blue Green	500	683	o	Dk. Yellow Beige	3045	888
✕	Dk. Blue Green	501	878	&	Pale Golden Brown	3827	311

BACKSTITCHES

SYMBOL	COLOR	DMC	ANCHOR
—	Black (2 str)	310	403
	- Shop names		
—	Lt. Steel Gray	318	399
	- All snow and ice		
—	Vy. Dk. Blue Green	500	683
	- All trees and borders		
—	Black Brown	3371	382
	- All else		

FRENCH KNOTS

SYMBOL	COLOR	DMC	ANCHOR
●	Black (2 str)	310	403
	- "i" dot		
●	Black Brown (2 str)	3371	382
	- Door latch, hinges and shutters		

Fabric: 14-count natural Aida
Stitch Count: 134 wide × 133 high

special instructions

Refer to pages 94-95 for general stitching information. Use 2 strands of floss for cross stitches and 1 strand for backstitches, unless otherwise noted.

HEMBLETON PEWTERER

FINISHED DESIGN SIZE: 8 1/2" X 8 3/8"
FRAME SIZE: 18 1/2" X 18 3/4"

HEMBLETON PEWTERER

ISSUED in 1992   RETIRED in 1995

The pewterer fashions and repairs
Our household goods, from pots to knives.
He works alone, yet surely shares
The dreams of other tradesmen's lives.

The sooty sweep, who all unseen,
Labors to keep the chimney clean,
Can, like the pewterer, know that he
Has given the world a finer sheen.

PERSONAL *Notes*

HEMBLETON PEWTERER

p a t t e r n

special instructions

Refer to pages 94-95 for general stitching
information. Use 2 strands of floss for cross
stitches and 1 strand for backstitches,
unless otherwise noted.

BLENDED STITCHES

÷ {	Pearl Gray (2 str)	415	398
	Silver blending filament (1 str)	001BF	001BF

BACKSTITCHES

—	Black (2 str) - Shop names	310	403
—	Black - Teapot on sign	310	403
—	Lt. Steel Gray - All snow and ice	318	399
—	Vy. Dk. Blue Green - All trees and borders	500	683
—	Black Brown - All else	3371	382

Fabric: 14-count natural Aida
Stitch Count: 121 wide × 120 high

THE PIED BULL INN

FINISHED DESIGN SIZE: 8 3/4" x 11 1/4"
FRAME SIZE: 19" x 22"

Dickens' Village Series

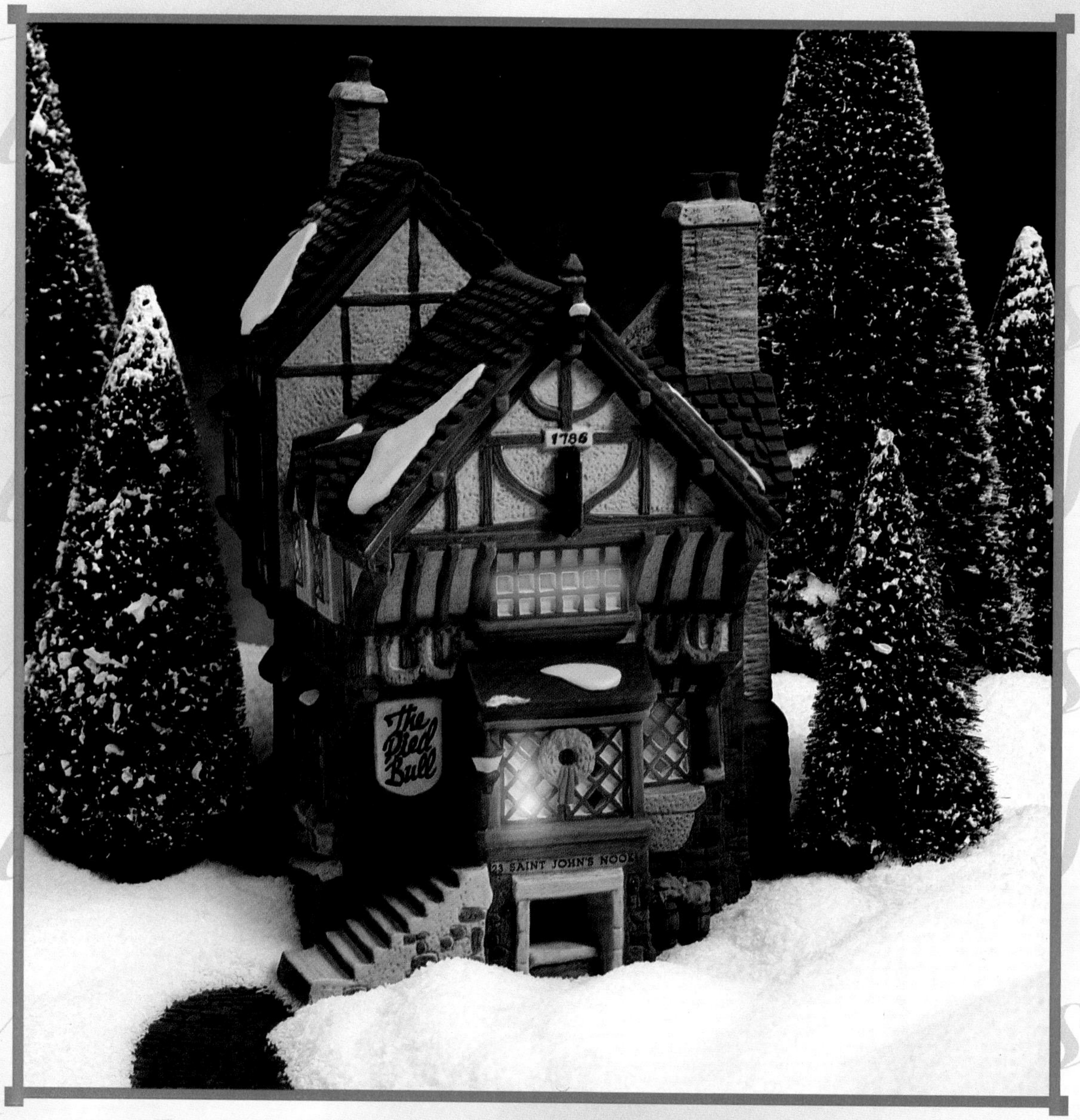

THE PIED BULL INN

ISSUED in 1993   RETIRED in 1993

LIMITED TO YEAR OF PRODUCTION

Steaming platters from the kitchen
Grace the laden table,
Savoury, hot, delicious—
Eat as much as you are able.
Quaff a pint of home-brewed ale,
Toast a new-found friend.
The Pied Bull's warmth and laughter
Signify your journey's end.

PERSONAL *Notes*

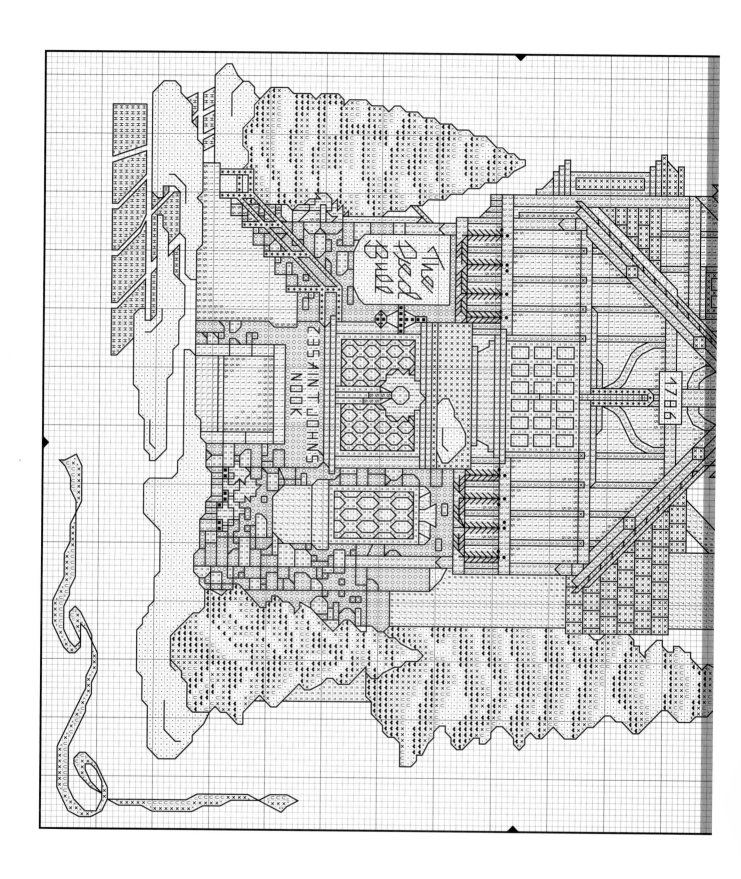

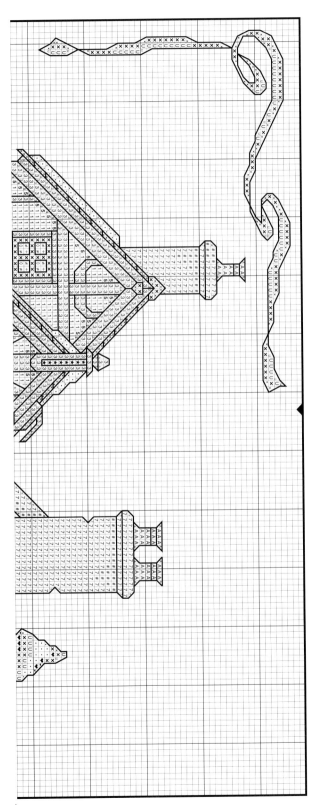

COLOR KEY

SYMBOL	COLOR	DMC	ANCHOR	SYMBOL	COLOR	DMC	ANCHOR
•	White	000	2	≠	Med. Yellow	743	302
s	Med. Christmas Red	304	1006	÷	Lt. Pale Yellow	745	300
■	Black	310	403	π	Dk. Beige Brown	839	360
H	Dk. Mahogany	400	351	‡	Dk. Emerald Green	910	229
L	Dk. Shell Gray	451	233	5	Vy. Lt. Brown Gray	3024	397
♣	Vy. Dk. Blue Green	500	683	#	Rose Brown	3064	883
×	Dk. Blue Green	501	878	3	Hunter Green	3346	267
u	Blue Green	502	877	★	Black Brown	3371	382
o	Vy. Dk. Rose Brown	632	936	7	Vy. Dk. Pink Beige	3773	1008
1	Ultra Vy. Lt. Tan	739	387	A	Terra Cotta	3830	5975
◇	Med. Tangerine	741	304				

BLENDED STITCHES

SYMBOL	COLOR	DMC	ANCHOR
+ {	Med. Old Gold (2 str)	729	890
{	Gold blending filament (1 str)	002BF	002BF

BACKSTITCHES

—	Black (2 str) - Inn names and numbers	310	403
—	Lt. Steel Gray - All snow and ice	318	399
—	Vy. Dk. Blue Green - All trees and borders	500	683
—	Dk. Emerald Green (2 str) - Garland and holly	910	229
—	Black Brown - All else	3371	382

FRENCH KNOTS

•	Med. Christmas Red (2 str) - Holly berries on garland	304	1006

special instructions

Refer to pages 94-95 for general stitching information. Use 2 strands of floss for cross stitches and 1 strand for backstitches, unless otherwise noted.

Fabric: 14-count natural Aida
Stitch Count: 129 wide × 164 high

GREAT DENTON MILL

FINISHED DESIGN SIZE: 8" x 10 1/4"
FRAME SIZE: 17 1/2" x 20 1/2"

GREAT DENTON MILL

ISSUED in 1993   CURRENT

A bubbling brook sends the wheel around,
Cogs clank and groan within;
Grinding oats and wheat into flour,
And carding wool to spin.

PERSONAL *Notes*

_____
_____
_____
_____
_____
_____
_____
_____
_____
_____
_____

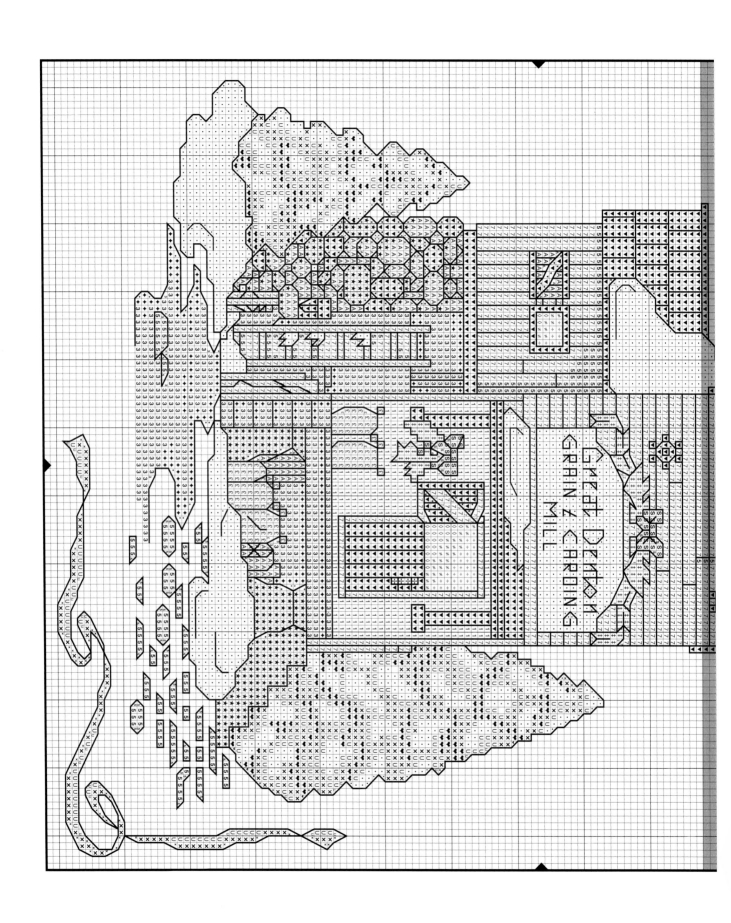

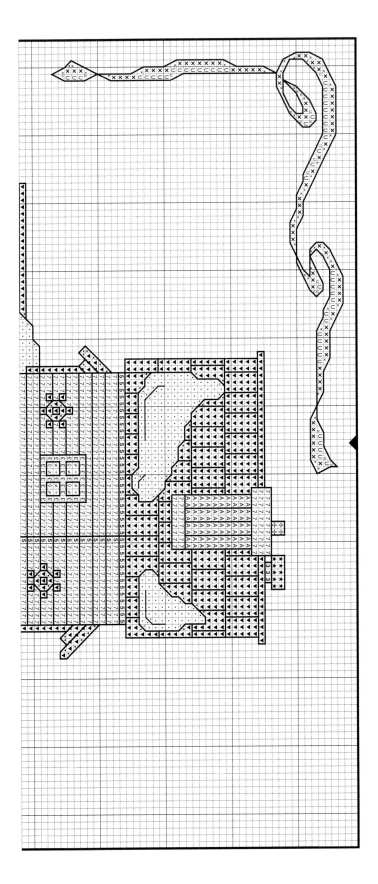

COLOR KEY

SYMBOL	COLOR	DMC	ANCHOR
•	White	000	2
s	Med. Christmas Red	304	1006
s	Pewter Gray	317	400
★	Vy. Dk. Blue Green	500	683
●	Dk. Blue Green	501	878
×	Blue Green	502	877
u	Ultra Vy. Lt. Beige Brown	543	933
1	Vy. Dk. Rose Brown	632	936
5	Med. Beaver Gray	647	1040

SYMBOL	COLOR	DMC	ANCHOR
3	Lt. Beaver Gray	648	900
◊	Med. Tangerine	741	304
≠	Med. Yellow	743	302
÷	Lt. Pale Yellow	745	300
‡	Dk. Emerald Green	910	229
▼	Ultra Dk. Coffee Brown	938	381
ε	Med. Golden Brown	976	1001
7	Dk. Rose Brown	3772	1007
A	Vy. Dk. Pink Beige	3773	1008

BLENDED STITCHES

SYMBOL	COLOR	DMC	ANCHOR
+ {	Pearl Gray (2 str)	415	398
	Silver blending filament (1 str)	001BF	001BF

BACKSTITCHES

SYMBOL	COLOR	DMC	ANCHOR
—	Black (2 str)	310	403
-	Mill name		
—	Lt. Steel Gray	318	399
—	- All snow and ice		
—	Vy. Dk. Blue Green	500	683
-	All trees and borders		
—	Black Brown	3371	382
-	All else		

Refer to pages 94-95 for general stitching information.

special instructions

Use 2 strands of floss for cross stitches and 1 strand for backstitches, unless otherwise noted.

Fabric: 14-count natural Aida
Stitch Count: 115 wide × 147 high

THE MERMAID FISH SHOPPE

FINISHED DESIGN SIZE: 83/8" X 91/8"
FRAME SIZE: 18" X 19"

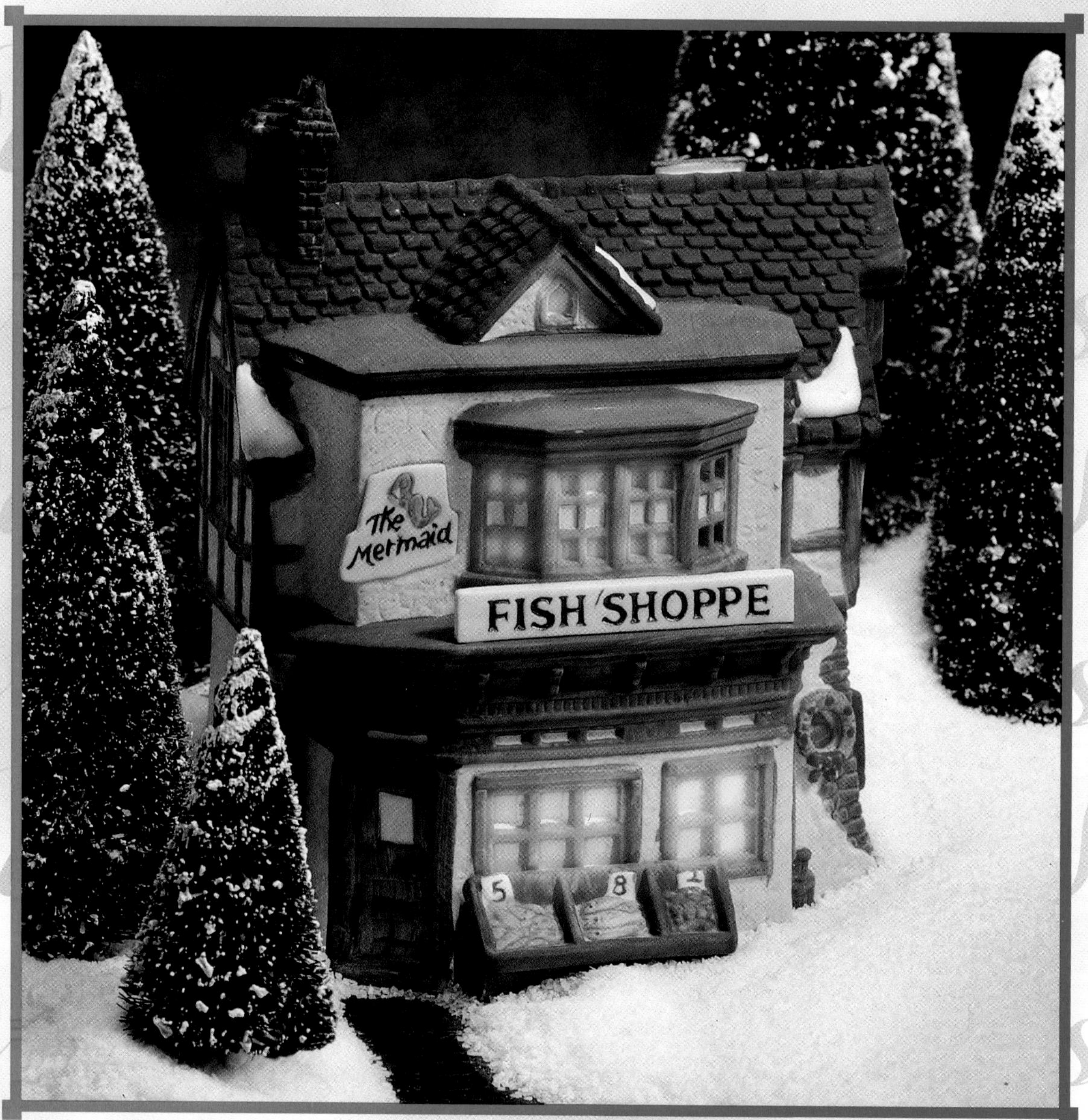
The Mermaid
FISH SHOPPE
5
8

THE MERMAID FISH SHOPPE

ISSUED in 1988   RETIRED in 1993

The treasures of the ocean,
Are vast and far below.
Its waters are a haven,
As tides do ebb and flow.

Dear to all good cooks,
Is the bounty from the blue.
At the Mermaid shoppe you'll find it,
For a perfect Codfish stew.

PERSONAL *Notes*

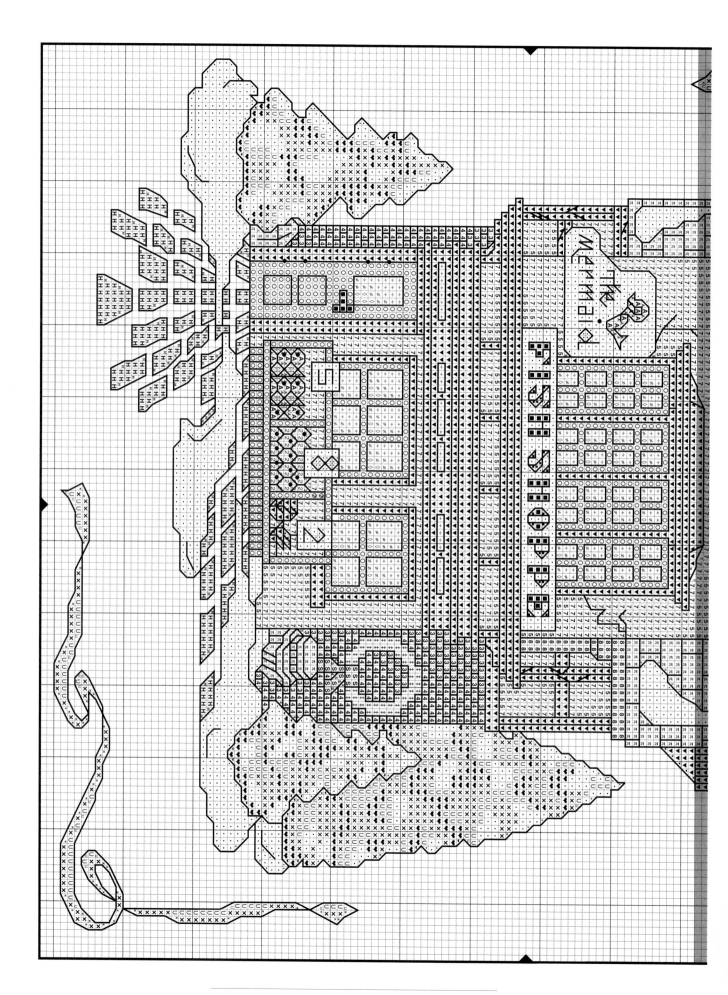

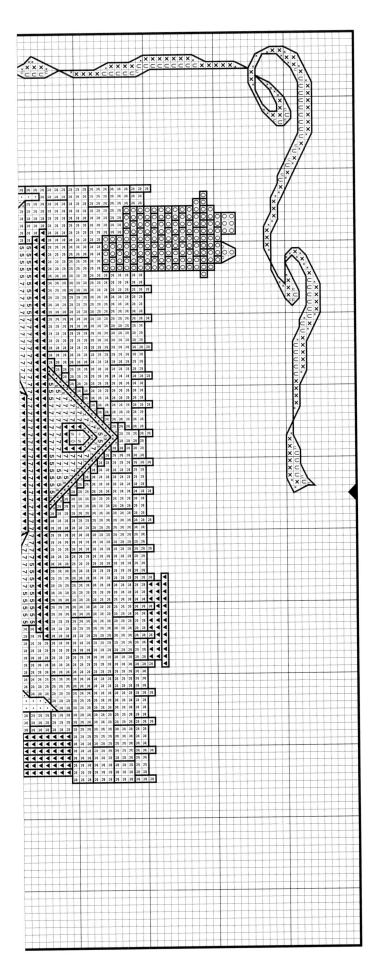

MERMAID FISH SHOPPE
p a t t e r n

COLOR KEY

SYMBOL	COLOR	DMC	ANCHOR	SYMBOL	COLOR	DMC	ANCHOR
•	White	000	2	÷	Lt. Pale Yellow	745	300
s	Med. Christmas Red	304	1006	‡	Dk. Emerald Green	910	229
■	Black	310	403	π	Red Copper	919	340
3	Med. Terra Cotta	356	5975	▼	Med. Avocado Green	937	268
8	Dk. Pewter Gray	413	401	7	Vy. Lt. Mocha Brown	3033	391
4	Tan	436	1045	o	Dk. Rose Brown	3772	1007
✦	Vy. Dk. Blue Green	500	683	2	Vy. Dk. Pink Beige	3773	1008
✕	Dk. Blue Green	501	878	5	Lt. Mocha Brown	3782	899
u	Blue Green	502	877	A	Aquamarine	3814	188
◇	Med. Tangerine	741	304	H	Terra Cotta	3830	5975
≠	Med. Yellow	743	302				

BACKSTITCHES

SYMBOL	COLOR	DMC	ANCHOR
—	Black (2 str)	310	403
	- Shop name, mermaid sign and prices		
—	Lt. Steel Gray	318	399
	- All snow and ice		
—	Vy. Dk. Blue Green	500	683
	- All trees and borders		
—	Black Brown	3371	382
	- All else		

FRENCH KNOTS

SYMBOL	COLOR	DMC	ANCHOR
•	Black	310	403
	"i" dot in Mermaid		
•	Black Brown - Fish eyes and door hinges	3371	382

Fabric: 14-count natural Aida
Stitch Count: 121 wide × 134 high

special instructions

Refer to pages 94-95 for general stitching information. Use 2 strands of floss for cross stitches and 1 strand for backstitches, unless otherwise noted.

OLD MICHAELCHURCH

FINISHED DESIGN SIZE: 9 1/4" x 12 1/8"
FRAME SIZE: 18 1/2" x 22"

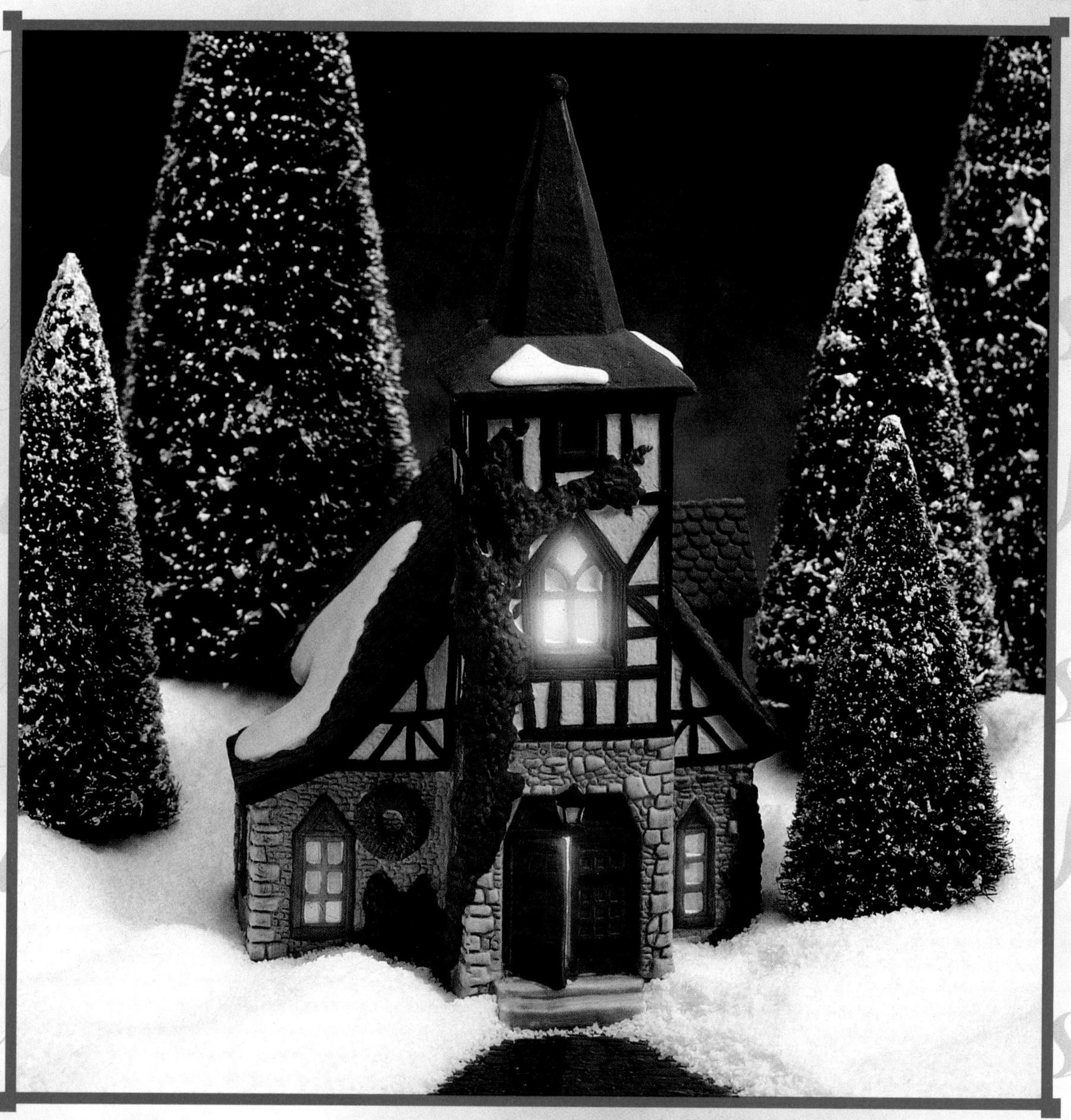

OLD MICHAELCHURCH

ISSUED in 1992   CURRENT

This ivy-covered Tudor church
Will open its doors wide
To share a blessing and a prayer
With those who come inside.

PERSONAL *Notes*

_____
_____
_____
_____
_____
_____
_____
_____
_____

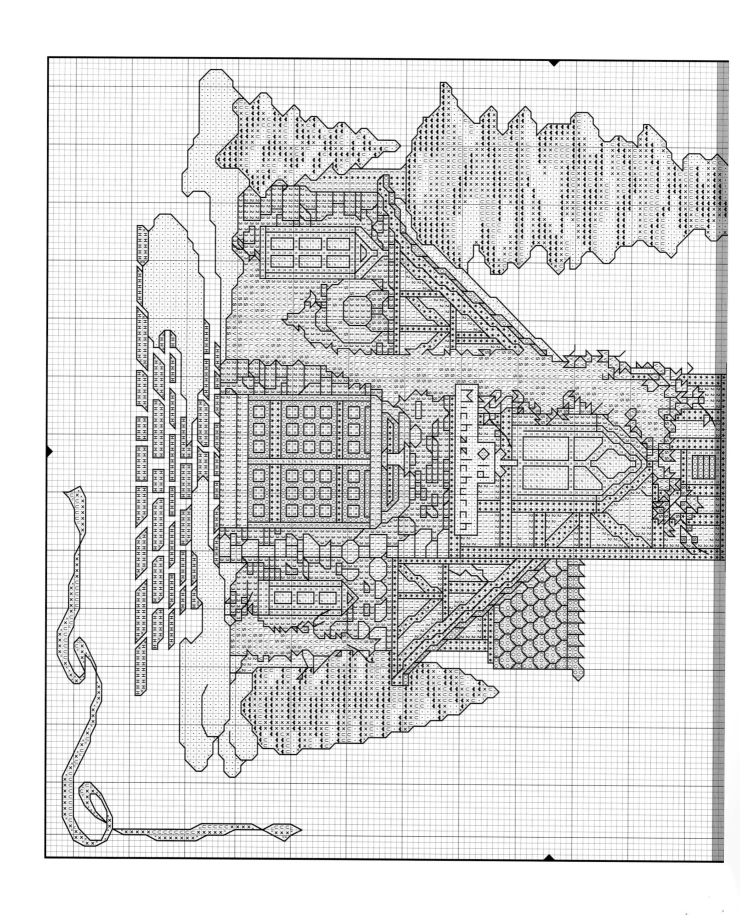

OLD MICHAELCHURCH
p a t t e r n

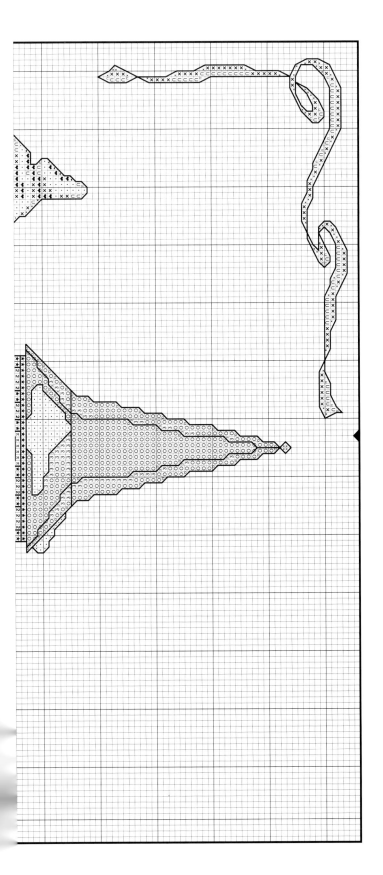

COLOR KEY

SYMBOL	COLOR	DMC	ANCHOR
•	White	000	2
s	Med. Christmas Red	304	1006
3	Dk. Shell Gray	451	233
2	Med. Shell Gray	452	232
1	Lt. Shell Gray	453	231
♥	Vy. Dk. Blue Green	500	683
×	Dk. Blue Green	501	878
u	Blue Green	502	877
ƒ	Vy. Dk. Rose Brown	632	936
◊	Med. Tangerine	741	304
≠	Med. Yellow	743	302
÷	Lt. Pale Yellow	745	300
★	Dk. Coffee Brown	801	359
‡	Dk. Emerald Green	910	229
L	Lt. Copper	922	1003
v	Med. Hunter Green	3347	266
o	Dk. Rose Brown	3772	1007
π	Lt. Mocha Brown	3782	899
H	Terra Cotta	3830	5975

BACKSTITCHES

SYMBOL	COLOR	DMC	ANCHOR
—	Black (2 str)	310	403
	- Church name		
—	Lt. Steel Gray	318	399
	- All snow and ice		
—	Vy. Dk. Blue Green	500	683
	- All trees and borders		
—	Black Brown	3371	382
	- All else		

Fabric: 14-count natural Aida
Stitch Count: 134 wide × 177 high

special instructions

Refer to pages 94-95 for general stitching information. Use 2 strands of floss for cross stitches and 1 strand for backstitches, unless otherwise noted.

FABRIC

Counted cross stitch uses fabrics that are evenly woven—the number of horizontal threads per inch (2.5 cm) should match the number of vertical threads per inch. If the fabric is not evenly woven, the design will be distorted. The Department 56 Village cross stitched models in this book were done on Charles Craft 14-count natural Aida, which means there are 14 threads to an inch (2.5 cm). Add at least 3" (7.5 cm) to all sides of the finished design size to determine the actual amount of fabric you will need. For example, if the finished design size is 10¼" × 12½" (26.1 × 31.8 cm) you will need to cut 16¼" × 18½" (41.1 × 47.3 cm).

Any even-weave fabric with a 14 count can be substituted for Aida. In addition, a 28-count fabric could be substituted, if you stitch over two threads instead of one. You can also change the size of a design by using a different-count fabric. This will change the amount of fabric needed, as well as the amount of floss.

To determine how much substitute fabric you will need, divide the stitch count width and height by the desired thread count. For example, if the stitch count is 143 × 176 squares, the finished design size will be 13" × 16" (33 × 40.5 cm) on 11-count fabric. This was determined by dividing 143 and 176 by 11. For 18-count fabric, dividing 143 and 176 by 18 means the design will be smaller, about 8" × 9¾" (20.5 × 25 cm).

The cut edges of even-weave fabrics will ravel, and they should be finished before stitching. Bind the edges with masking tape, apply liquid fray preventer, or sew the edges with a zigzag or overcast stitch. The last method is recommended for projects of heirloom quality. Use an embroidery hoop or scroll frame while stitching to keep the fabric taut.

FLOSS

Two brands of floss are listed on the Color Key. It is recommended that you do not mix floss brands. The Department 56 Village cross stitched models in this book were done with DMC floss.

Cut floss strands about 18" (46 cm). Separate all floss strands, and then put the appropriate number back together. To separate floss strands, begin pulling the strands apart in the center of the 18" (46 cm) length and work out to the ends. Use two strands of floss for the cross stitches, and one strand for backstitches, unless noted differently.

FINDING THE CENTER OF THE FABRIC

All designs are centered on the fabric; to find the center, fold the fabric in half from top to bottom and then in half again from side to side. Gently pinch the fabric along the folds to make slight creases, which will intersect at the center point. Mark the center with a straight pin or basting lines.

DESIGN CHART

Each square on a chart represents one cross stitch, and each cross stitch is worked over one thread. The symbols on the chart represent the color of a stitch. The Color Key indicates which color the symbol represents. Special instructions for each design, such as backstitch colors and special stitches, are noted within the Color Key.

BEGINNING STITCHING

Cut the appropriate color floss, separate the strands and put two of them back together. Thread floss through the needle, and bring the needle up through the fabric from the back side. Leave a small tail of floss, and hold it in place as you work the first few stitches over the tail. Do not knot the floss.

Kreinik® blending filaments are used to achieve special effects, such as metallic finishes. Blending filaments and embroidery floss have different elasticities. To deal with that difference, it is recommended that you knot the blending filament on the needle. Pass a loop of blending filament through the eye of the needle; then insert the point of the needle through the loop. Tighten the loop at the end of the eye. Thread other floss through the eye of the needle to begin stitching (PHOTO 1).

PHOTO 1

CROSS STITCHING

There are four small open spaces surrounding each fabric thread. To make a single cross stitch, bring the needle up at 1 and down at 2, up at 3 and down at 4 (PHOTO 2). To make several cross stitches in a row, work the first half of the stitches in one direction, and the other half in the opposite direction. For an expert finish, the top stitch in all cross stitches should go in the same direction. Make certain that your stitches are taut, but not so tight that the fabric threads are pulled out of shape. Work rows in a downward direction; this keeps stitches smoother. You can turn the fabric and the chart upside down, if necessary.

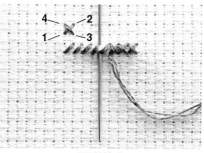
PHOTO 2

Complete all the cross stitches first, working from the center outward; then follow the special instructions to complete the design with details such as backstitching or special stitches. In these designs, ¼ and ¾ cross stitches are used to make fine details, curved lines and special shading effects (PHOTO 3). A ¼ cross stitch is represented on the chart with a smaller symbol from the Color Key in the corner needed. A ¾ cross stitch is represented with a small symbol in the corner plus a diagonal line. Each of these stitches can go in any of four different directions, depending on the side of the diagonal line and the corner on which the symbol is printed. For the ¾ cross stitch, stitch a ¼ cross stitch of floss color, and the ½ cross stitch in the same color. If the ¾ cross

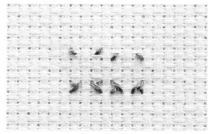
PHOTO 3

stitch has a backstitch across it, that will be the ½ cross stitch.

SPECIAL STITCHES

Detail and definition are created by outlining with the backstitch (PHOTO 4). French knots add punctuation on signs or other highlights, and are done as shown. Using the number of strands indicated, bring the needle up through the fabric hole. Holding the thread taut, wrap the needle by passing the thread over and under in a spiral motion. Holding the remaining thread firmly, insert the needle into the fabric close to the hole where it started. Tug the thread until excess is pulled through.

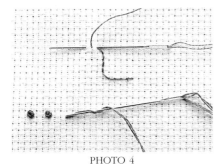

PHOTO 4

ENDING STITCHING

When you have completed all adjoining stitches with one color, fasten the floss and begin with the next color as described above. To fasten the floss, bring the floss to the back side and run under at least four stitches to hold it in place. Clip the floss close to the fabric; do not knot (PHOTO 5).

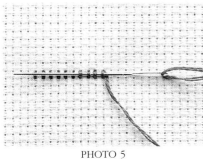

PHOTO 5

Even though the same color of floss is used on another part of the design, you should fasten the floss and start again in the new spot. Floss that is run across the back of the fabric from one spot to another will often show through on the front.

FINISHING

Lay the stitched piece facedown on a terry-cloth towel. Dampen it slightly if it is badly creased. Press from the wrong side with a medium-hot iron. If the piece has become soiled, it can be soaked in cold water with a mild detergent. However, you should test the floss for colorfastness before washing your completed piece. Do not wring out the fabric. Roll it in terry-cloth towels to remove excess moisture, and press on the wrong side until it is dry.

STRETCHING AND MOUNTING

Matting and framing your Department 56 design will offer protection to the piece. A single mat is usually all that is needed to raise the glass in a frame above the surface of the stitching. Spacers should be used if framing is done without a mat. For the best protection of all projects, use acid-free foam-core boards and mat boards.

To frame the stitched design without any wrinkles or bubbles, the fabric is stretched around a foam-core mounting board. For easy mounting, 3" (7.5 cm) of fabric were allowed on each side of the design. If necessary, fabric strips can be stitched to the sides of the design if you were not able to work with a piece of fabric that size.

Cut the acid-free foam-core mounting board with a utility knife and straightedge at least 2" (5 cm) larger than the image opening of the mat. This allows you to adjust the position of the mounting board behind the mat. If a mat is not desired, the mounting board is cut to fit the frame opening.

Center the design right side up over foam-core board. Insert a T-pin through the fabric and into the edge of the foam core, at the center of one side. Aligning the grain of the fabric with the edge of the board, pin the fabric at each corner of that side, pulling the fabric taut between pins. Repeat to stretch and

PHOTO 6

pin the fabric to the adjacent side, then the remaining sides (PHOTO 6).

Continue to stretch and pin the fabric between T-pins, completing one side at a time and spacing T-pins every ½" (1.3 cm). Recheck that the design is straight; repin as necessary. Check that the fabric is taut by smoothing a finger across the piece; you should not be able to push any excess fabric. Repin the fabric as necessary (PHOTO 7).

PHOTO 7

Sequin pins are recommended to secure the fabric to the mounting board; they will not damage the fabric and can be removed if you wish to use the piece for another project at a later date. Insert the sequin pins into the edge of the board at ¼" (6 mm) intervals, removing the T-pins.

Fold in the excess fabric at the corners; secure with hand stitching. Your stretched cross stitch design is now ready to be matted or framed (PHOTO 8).

PHOTO 8

Credits

CY DECOSSE INCORPORATED
President/COO: Nino Tarantino
Executive V.P./Editor-in-Chief: William B. Jones
Chairman Emeritus: Cy DeCosse

Group Executive Editor: Zoe A. Graul
Associate Creative Director: Lisa Rosenthal
Art Director: Stephanie Michaud
Project Manager: Amy Berndt
Sample Production Manager: Carol Olson
Technical Editor: Deborah Howe
Editor: Janice Cauley
Contributing Writer: Barbara Lund
Contributing Artists: Eileen Bovard, Gerald Goodge
Project Stylist: Christine Jahns
Technical Photo Stylists: Bridget Haugh, Coralie Sathre,
  Nancy Sundeen
Styling Director: Bobbette Destiche
Prop Stylists: Elizabeth Emmons, Christine Jahns, Michele Joy
Food Stylists: Elizabeth Emmons, Nancy Johnson
Artisans: Arlene Dohrman, Phyllis Galbraith, Carol Pilot,
  Michelle Skudlarek
Vice President of Photography & Production: Jim Bindas
Creative Photo Coordinator: Cathleen Shannon
Studio Manager: Marcia Chambers
Photographers: Mark Macemon, Michael Parker,
  Steve Smith
Print Production Manager: Mary Ann Knox
Senior Desktop Publishing Specialist: Joe Fahey
Desktop Publishing Specialist: Laurie Kristensen
Production Staff: Kathlynn Henthorne, Laura Hokkanen,

Tom Hoops, Mark Jacobson, Jeanette Moss, Mike Schauer,
  Michael Sipe, Brent Thomas, Greg Wallace, Kay Wethern
Shop Supervisor: Phil Juntti
Scenic Carpenters: Troy Johnson, Rob Johnstone, John Nadeau
Contributors: Crescent Matboard Co., The DMC Corporation,
  EZ International
Pattern Conversions: The Design Connection, Inc.

COWLES
Enthusiast Media

President/COO: Philip L. Penny

Printed on American paper by:
  R. R. Donnelley & Sons Co. (0796)
99 98 97 96 / 5 4 3 2 1

Cy DeCosse Incorporated offers a variety of how-to books.
For information write:
  Cy DeCosse Subscriber Books
  5900 Green Oak Drive
  Minnetonka, MN 55343

Also available from The Heritage Village Collection® cross stitch pattern books:
The North Pole© Series, The New England Village® Series and The Christmas in the City® Series.

The designs in this book are brought to life in Department 56®, Inc.'s Dickens' Village Series®
of handcrafted, lighted porcelain houses, buildings and coordinated accessories.

The Finished Design Size is an actual measurement of the Department 56® Village cross stitched models
featured in this book, and should be used as an approximation. Your Finished Design Size may vary depending
on the type and brand of fabric used, stitching ability or blocking method, along with other factors.

For more information about the Dickens' Village Series® and the entire
Heritage Village Collection® of fine quality porcelain collectibles, or to find the Department 56®, Inc.
authorized village dealer nearest you, contact:

Department 56
INC.

ONE VILLAGE PLACE
6436 CITY WEST PARKWAY
EDEN PRAIRIE, MN 55344

1-800-LIT-TOWN
(548-8696)